Field Guide
to
Bible
Promises
True Stories for Real Kids

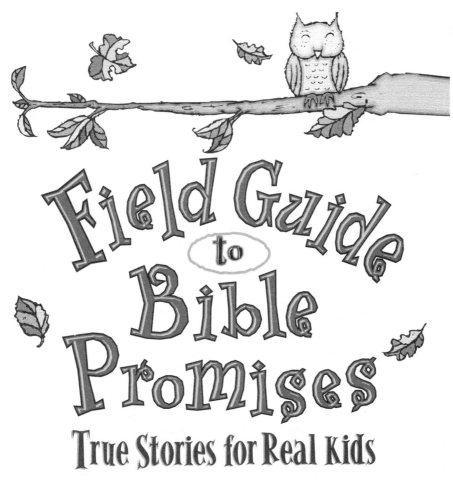

Field Guide to Bible Promises

True Stories for Real Kids

by HELEN HAIDLE

illustrated by mARTiN lemmelMAN

Zonderkidz

The children's group of Zondervan

Zonder**kidz**™

The children's group of Zondervan

Field Guide to Bible Promises
Copyright © 2001 by Helen Haidle
Illustrations, copyright © 2001 by Martin Lemmelman

Requests for information shoud be addressed to:

Zonderkidz, *Grand Rapids, Michigan 49530*
www.zonderkidz.com

Zonderkidz is a trademark of Zondervan.

ISBN 0-310-70037-X

Editor: Gwen Ellis
Art Production and Design: Jody Langley
Illustration: Martin Lemmelman

Printed in the United States

01 02 03 04 /❖ DC/ 10 9 8 7 6 5 4 3 2 1

This book is dedicated to the people who shared their
experiences on which these stories were based:
Brittany Nigro, Michael Koch, Irena Koch Durrant,
John Bennett, Brother David in China, Linda Jean Sattgast,
Barbara Martin, Jeannie St. John Taylor.

And to Nyla Booth, Ann Scott, and Cammi Scott (From their
book Room for One More, published by Tyndale House, 1984).

H.H.—

In memory of Matt Kush.
"We will always remember your smile."

M.L.—

In appreciation to:

Barbara Martin, Monica Piatt, and Jeannie St. John Taylor, who read this manuscript while it was in process and gave their valuable critiques and suggestions.

CONTENTS

Chapter 1

Guess What? God Still Keeps Every Promise!

The World's Greatest Treasure

What would you consider to be the greatest treasure in the whole world?

- The jeweled crowns that belong to the queen of England?

- An old pirate's chest full of gold coins and jewels?

- A diamond mine?

Think about all the "earthly treasures" in your own house and your own bedroom. What is the most important thing you own?

Don't Miss the Treasure!

Sometimes people have thrown away a great treasure without knowing it.

Many years ago in South Africa, there lived a man who owned a large ranch. But even though he possessed many cattle and a lot of land, he was not happy. More than anything else, he dreamed of finding diamonds.

So one day he sold his land and gave up ranching.

The man traveled many years, searching in faraway places. He looked everywhere for a diamond mine. But he never found one.

He finally used up all of his money. And he had nothing at all to show for the money he spent. Now he didn't own anything at all. He died penniless.

In the meantime, the person who bought this man's ranch took good care of the cattle and other animals. He spent time fixing up the buildings and the fences.

The new man also did some digging in one section of the ranch. And guess what? He discovered a diamond mine.

In fact, it turned out that he discovered the world's largest diamond mine! And now he was the owner of that entire fortune because it was all on his land.

Without knowing it, the first owner had given away the very thing he longed for—a valuable diamond mine. It had been right in his own backyard while he looked everywhere else!

What About You?

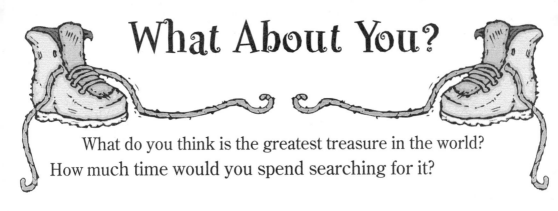

What do you think is the greatest treasure in the world? How much time would you spend searching for it?

How would you start looking for a treasure?

Would you search for some old writings or maps that could help you find information on the greatest treasure in the world?

Would you look through old ship records and search the bottom of the ocean if you knew you would find a long-lost ship and its cargo of gold?

How much time and money would you be willing to spend to discover a great treasure?

You can be sure that God doesn't want to hide any great treasures from the people he loves.

In fact, God wants you to find a great treasure. God desires for you to own this treasure. God delights in giving you many treasures. They are for you to use. And God wants you to enjoy all the treasure he gives.

Now come and discover this treasure. For God has put the world's greatest treasure in a simple place where anyone can find it.

Do you know where that might be?

You don't have to guess or wonder where the greatest treasure in the world is. God tells us where to find it. This rich treasure is found in the pages of a book.

The treasure is worth much more than thousands of pieces of gold and silver. And you can have it . . . and own it . . . for free! But instead of digging through dirt, you have to "dig" deep through pages of paper.

And when you find treasure, it will be yours.

You've probably guessed which book contains this treasure. Yes, it is in the Bible, God's own Word!

As you read the Bible, you will receive the treasure of God's great promises!

This is what King David said to God:

How sweet are your words to my taste,
sweeter than honey to my mouth! . . .
The law from your mouth is more precious
to me than thousands of pieces
of silver and gold.

Psalm 119:103, 72

What Is a Promise?

A promise is made when someone says he will do something for you or with you. When someone gives you a promise, he wants you to trust him.

You expect a promise to be kept. But often people break their promises. And sometimes promises cannot be kept because of bad weather, sickness, or accidents.

A promise is only as good as the person who makes it. You can't trust a liar to keep a promise.

Think about the people who have made promises to you. If they are people who tell the truth, you can feel confident they will keep their promise.

Do you know why God's promises are so valuable? It's because God keeps every promise.

Be glad that you never have to wonder if God will keep his promises. You can always count on God to do what he says. When you learn God's promises, you will learn to know what God is like. And God is totally trustworthy.

King Solomon, the wisest man who ever lived, knew this was true. Solomon wrote,

> Trust in the Lord with all your heart and lean not on your own understanding.
>
> Proverbs 3:5

Find the Greatest Treasure!

The world's greatest treasure can be found right in your own house—or on a shelf in your own bedroom. Great treasures are hidden just inside your Bible.

God promises, "You will seek me and find me when you seek me with all your heart" (Jeremiah 29:13).

Don't miss out on finding God and knowing him! Then go on a treasure hunt for God's promises.

Dig for them. Write them down. See how many you can find. If you take time and make the effort, you will discover the riches hidden in the Bible. You will get to know God, and you will learn to trust that God keeps every promise. What a treasure!

But you'll never search for God's promises unless you are convinced they are much better than the finest gold.

King David knew the value of God's Word and promises. He wrote, "I love your commands more than gold, more than pure gold" (Psalm 119:127).

God, and his Word and promises, are more valuable than all the diamonds or gold in the entire world!

These great treasures will freely be given to all who seek to know God. This book will be like a map to point you to God's treasure. Come and discover the promises of God. Read the amazing stories of how God has kept his promises in the past and still keeps them today. So come and dig in—it will be worth it!

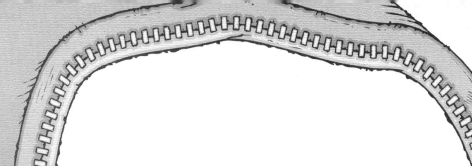

Chapter 2

God's Promise:
I Will Take Care
of You

KNOCK! KNOCK! KNOCK!

A fist pounded on the door of a small home in China.

Chung's heart raced as he glanced out the window and saw two police vans parked in front of the house, and a group of Chinese police standing at the front door.

"Don't worry," said his father in a low voice. "Keep calm. God will take care of us." He slowly opened the door and faced an angry police officer.

"We warned you and your wife to stop teaching people lies about God," said the officer. "But you haven't stopped! Now you are under arrest!"

The officers grabbed Chung's father and mother and pushed them into the van. Chung watched it drive away. While Chung held the hands of his younger brother and sister, trying to comfort them, three officers searched the house.

The police took all the money they found. They emptied the kitchen cupboards and carried the food, along with a table and four chairs, out to a second van.

Then Chung heard the police threatening neighbors who had gathered in the street. They yelled, "Have nothing to do with these children! Their parents are enemies of the state. Don't help them—or you will be arrested, too!"

After the police left, Chung and his brother and sister sat down on the floor and cried.

"Dear God," prayed Chung quietly. "We trust you to take care of us. Please take care of Dad and Mom, too. Bring them back home soon."

Chung's little sister tugged at his sleeve. "I'm hungry," she said. "What are we going to eat?"

"Don't you remember?" he said. "The police took everything. They even emptied the rice out of our rice pot into their sack. There is nothing left."

The little girl burst into tears. "But my stomach hurts!"

Chung held the big rice pot in front of her. "Look inside!" he said impatiently. "It's empty."

"Oh!" she exclaimed. "There's some left!"

Chung tipped the jar upside down on the counter. A cupful of rice spilled out—just enough for one meal. He cooked it on the stove and then scooped it into three bowls. Mouths watering, the children knelt down and prayed, "Thank you, God, for taking care of us. Thank you for this rice."

They ate it eagerly. Afterward, exhausted by the day's trouble, they fell asleep.

The next morning the little ones woke Chung.

"We're hungry!" they said with tears in their eyes.

Chung's stomach ached, too. "The rice is gone," he said firmly. "We ate it last night."

His sister headed for the kitchen.

Chung shouted after her, "The rice pot is empty!" He couldn't help but feel upset and worried. How was he going to take care of the little ones? There was no money left to buy food.

Then he heard a squeal from the kitchen.

"Come look inside! There's a little bit left!"

And sure enough, there was a little bit left. And that's the way it went. Every time the children needed to eat, they found just enough rice in the pot for their next meal.

Ten days later the children's parents were released from prison.

"God answered our prayers," Chung told them. "God took care of us. We always had just enough rice for one more meal."

Chung and his brother and sister never forgot how God took care of them when they couldn't take care of themselves.

What About You?

What do you worry about the most?

Do you worry about being hungry?

Do you worry about your schoolwork?

Are you afraid something will happen to your family?

Or do you worry that other kids will not like you?

Parents worry, too. They worry about having enough money to buy food and to pay bills. Sometimes they worry about losing a job. What would you say to someone who felt worried?

Do you know what Jesus said about worry?

Jesus said, "Do not worry about your life, what you will eat or drink; or about your body, what you will wear.... Look at the birds of the air; they do not sow or reap or store away in barns."

Do you think Jesus wants you to worry?

Jesus told his disciples, "Your heavenly Father feeds the birds. Are you not much more valuable than they?" (Matthew 6:25–26).

Turn the page and read about how God once used some birds to help take care of a man.

God Took Care of Elijah
1 Kings 17

Long ago there was a great famine in the land of Israel. No rain fell for three years. No plants grew.

Ahab, the king of Israel, blamed the prophet Elijah for the famine. He wanted to kill Elijah.

So God told Elijah to go and live by a small brook far out in the country, where he would be safe.

God promised, "You shall drink from the water of the brook, and I will send ravens to feed you there."

Every morning and every evening, the black ravens flew to Elijah and gave him bread and meat to eat.

God kept his promise to take care of Elijah.

Then one day the water in the brook dried up from lack of rain. God told Elijah, "Go to Zarephath. A widow in that place will give you food to eat."

When Elijah found the woman he asked her,

"Would you please bring me a drink. And a piece of bread, too?"

"I don't have any bread," the woman told Elijah. "All I have is a little flour in a jar and a little olive oil in a jug. I'm getting ready to make one last meal for my son and myself. After we eat it, we will die."

"Don't be afraid," Elijah said. "First make some bread for me. Then make some for you and your son.

"The Lord, who is the God of Israel, gives you this promise: 'The jar of flour will not be used up. The jug will always have oil in it. You will have flour and oil until the day the Lord sends rain.'"

The woman discovered that God keeps his promises. All the time she made bread for Elijah, her jar of flour never ran out. And her jug always had oil in it.

All during the time of great famine, God supplied food for Elijah, the widow, and her son.

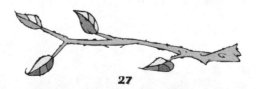

What Does This Mean for You?

To Think About:

- When has God taken care of you?

- What are some ways in which God cares for you each day?

- Was there ever a time when God took care of you in a way that was different from what you prayed for or expected?

ALWAYS REMEMBER

- You are God's dear child. Don't worry. Trust God's care. God is concerned about every detail of your life.

- God will give you all that you need. But God may not give you everything you want. (God gave Elijah just enough bread for one day. The Chinese children had just enough rice for each meal. God did not give them cake and ice cream!)

- You are God's child, and you can be sure he will take care of you. Isn't that wonderful! And because God loves you so much, you will want to put him first in your life.

GOD'S TREASURY OF PROMISES

Cast all your anxiety on God
because he cares for you.
1 Peter 5:7

The Lord is good. . . .
He cares for those who trust in him.
Nahum 1:7

God will meet all your needs according
to his glorious riches in Christ Jesus.
Philippians 4:19

Do not worry, saying, "What shall we eat?" . . .
Your heavenly Father knows what you need.
Matthew 6:31—32

Seek first God's kingdom and his righteousness,
and all these things will be given to you as well.
Matthew 6:33

They will neither hunger nor thirst,
nor will the desert heat or the sun beat upon them.
He who has compassion on them will guide them
and lead them beside springs of water.
Isaiah 49:10

He fulfills the desires of those who fear him;
he hears their cry and saves them.
Psalms 145:19

The gracious hand of our God
is on everyone who looks to him."
Ezra 8:22

The poor will see and be glad—
you who seek the God, may your hearts live!
Psalms 69:32

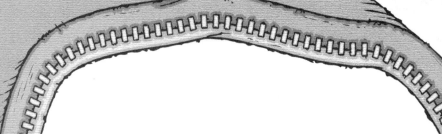

Chapter 3

God's Promise:
I Will Listen When
You Pray

T revor burst through the front door, through the living room, and into the kitchen, yelling loudly, "Dad! Mom! Come quick—Jeremiah is missing!"

His parents were preparing dinner. Dad looked up and said, "Calm down. What happened?"

"All the kids in the neighborhood were playing hide-and-seek. Jeremiah tagged along and wanted to join us. At first I wouldn't let him. But he kept begging until I did," explained Trevor. He wiped his forehead and gulped down a glass of lemonade.

"When the game ended, everyone came out of hiding … except for Jeremiah. We can't find him!"

Trevor's dad put an arm around his son. Tears ran down Trevor's cheeks, and he said, "I feel terrible! It's all my fault that Jeremiah is missing."

"First of all, it's not your fault," said Mother. "His parents must be frantic. We'd better get out there and help search for him."

"They're putting together search parties now. They need people to help look for him. I've got to help them. No time for supper."

"I'll help, too," Dad said, grabbing a jacket. "We've got to hurry. It will be dark in a couple of hours."

Trevor and his dad hurried down the block to their neighbor's house. They prayed as they ran.

"Bless these parents, dear God," prayed Dad. "Give them peace in their hearts. Help us find Jeremiah."

Trevor added, "Oh, God, please take care of little Jeremiah. Keep him safe."

By the time they got to Jeremiah's home, the police had arrived and were organizing search parties. Trevor and his dad looked at the map the police had laid out and volunteered to search the wooded hill at the end of the block.

"Hurry, Dad," said Trevor as they scrambled up the rocky slope. "We don't have much time before sunset. After that it will be impossible to see anything—especially a little three-year-old kid."

"Right," agreed Dad. "His mom said he was only wearing a short-sleeved shirt. Temperatures are going to drop below freezing tonight."

Calling for Jeremiah, they searched behind every bush and boulder where a three-year-old could hide.

"Do you think he climbed this far?" asked Trevor. "Wouldn't he be crying for help?"

Dad nodded. "Maybe he has been crying. His voice could be all worn out by now."

The sky was turning purple by the time they worked their way to the top of the hill. "It's time to go back, Trevor," said Dad quietly. "At least we have to go back and get a flashlight."

Trevor pulled his father's sleeve. "Wait, Dad," he begged. "I can't leave yet. Let's pray once more."

He knelt right down in the dirt, and his dad joined him.

"O Lord, you're the only one who knows where Jeremiah is.

Where should we look?" pleaded Trevor. "Help us find him before we go back."

Trevor slowly stood up. All at once he noticed a small trail.

"Wait, Dad. Let me check this out. If I were a little kid, I'd follow this trail." Trevor got down on his hands and knees and crawled into the thick brush.

The trail ended only a few feet into the bushes. As Trevor turned to go back, he heard a noise like a kitten's meow. He pulled aside some brush and saw two little feet. "Jeremiah!" he cried happily.

The child's tired voice let out a raspy squeak. He couldn't talk, but he held out his arms to Trevor. Trevor scooped the little boy up in his arms and hugged him. "Don't be afraid, Jeremiah. I'll take you home."

As Trevor's dad carried the little boy down the hill, Trevor wondered, *If we hadn't stopped to pray, what would have happened?*

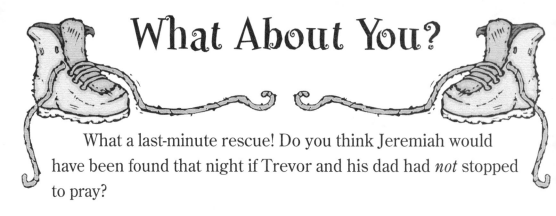

What About You?

What a last-minute rescue! Do you think Jeremiah would have been found that night if Trevor and his dad had *not* stopped to pray?

What about the last time you needed help? Did you go to your parents or your teacher or a friend ... *before* you prayed to God?

Do you really believe God hears and answers every prayer?

What will you do in the future when you have a need?

Did Jesus ever refuse to help anyone who asked?

Did he get irritated at people who came to him with a problem?

Think about people in the Bible who prayed. Once a father asked Jesus to come to his house and heal his sick daughter. Mary and Martha asked Jesus to help their sick brother. Outcast lepers asked Jesus to have mercy on them and heal them.

Here is the story of a woman who realized no one could help her except God. Find out how God answered her prayers.

God Answered Hannah's Prayers
1 Samuel 1:1-2:11, 18-21

More than anything, Hannah wanted a baby.
Every day she felt sad and tears ran down her
cheeks. She knew that her husband, Elkanah,
loved her very much. He tried to comfort
Hannah. But the hurt in her heart didn't go away.

One day when Hannah went to the house of
the Lord, she stood by the door and prayed
earnestly.

While she prayed, Hannah cried. She made a
promise to the Lord, saying, "Lord, please give
me a son. If you do, I'll give him back to you. He
will serve you all of his life."

Eli, the priest, saw Hannah crying and thought
she must have had too much to drink. He said to
her, "Get rid of your wine. Stop getting drunk."

She told him, "I haven't been drinking. I'm
praying because I'm very sad. I was telling the
Lord all of my sorrows."

Eli blessed her and said, "Go in peace. May the God of Israel give you what you have asked."

Then Hannah left. She smiled because she was no longer sad. She believed God would answer her prayers.

In a few months Hannah had a baby boy. She named him Samuel.

When Samuel was about three or four years old, Hannah brought him to Eli. She told Eli, "I'm the woman who once stood here beside you and prayed for this child, and the Lord gave him to me. Now I'm giving him back to the Lord."

It was hard for Hannah to give up the thing she loved most. So every year when Hannah went to the house of the Lord, she brought Samuel a little robe she had made.

The Lord was good to Hannah. Her son grew up to be a great prophet and a great leader of the people of Israel. And the Lord also gave Hannah *more* than she asked for—three more sons and two daughters!

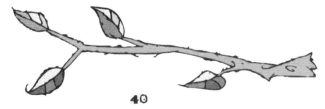

What Does This Mean for You?

To Think About:

- What prayer has God answered for you?

- What are you praying about today?

- Are you trusting God to do the best thing in your life?

- Has there been a time when God gave you something different from what you asked?

- Was there ever a time when you received more than you had asked from God?

ALWAYS REMEMBER

- God does not get tired of people who pray. God is never bothered by prayer. God invites us to pray.

- Nothing is too hard for God. So be glad and trust God as you pray. Know that God hears and will answer every one of your prayers. Look for God's answers.

- God doesn't promise to give you exactly what you ask. You may expect God to answer your prayers in a certain way, but God may have another way. And God may give you more than you ask!

GOD'S TREASURY OF PROMISES

The Lord says, "Call to me and I will answer you and tell you great and unsearchable things you do not know."
Jeremiah 33:3

The arm of the Lord is not too short to save, nor his ear too dull to hear.
Isaiah 59:1

Jesus said, "If you remain in me and my words remain in you, ask whatever you wish, and it will be given you."
John 15:7

Jesus said, "If you . . . know how to give good gifts to your children, how much more will your Father in heaven give good gifts to those who ask him!"
Matthew 7:11

This is the confidence we have in approaching God: that if we ask anything according to his will, he hears us. And if we know that he hears us—whatever we ask—we know that we have what we asked of him.
1 John 5:14–15

Chapter 4

God's Promise:
I Will Make You
Strong and Brave

"Mom! This old house smells funny," said Michael as he peered down the dark basement stairway. "Are you sure there are no bugs or spiders here?"

Michael hated insects. He couldn't stand anything that crawled. And he wasn't happy about his family's latest move—to the old brick house that belonged to their church.

Michael's dad had left their family a year ago, and now they had run out of money. So the local church members let Michael, his mother, and his four brothers and sisters live in the house.

Mother handed a cardboard box to Michael with a smile and said, "Quit worrying, Son. Let's get the car unloaded. Just concentrate on setting up your new bedroom. And remember, God gave us this house to live in, so God will just have to help us live here . . . even if some bugs show up."

Michael took the box upstairs to his attic room. He groaned as he noticed a spiderweb above his doorway. He stopped long enough to knock it down and to silently pray, *Oh, dear God, why did you make insects—especially spiders? Help me deal with this.*

When Michael woke up the next morning, he looked out the small window of the attic. He could see blue sky through the branches of an old oak tree. A bird's nest perched on the tall branches. *Maybe this won't be so bad after all*, he thought.

Suddenly he gasped!

There on the window's lacy white curtain was a black spot, and it was moving. It was a great big ugly spider. Michael wanted to scream but couldn't.

Just then the door of his room opened and his mother came into the room. He heard her gasp and knew that she, too, had seen the spider. As they watched, the spider crawled higher up the curtain. Soon it would be on the wall and then would climb up out of reach. They had to do something quickly.

Michael looked at his mother. Her white face and wide-eyed stare told him she didn't like spiders any more than he did.

He grabbed a magazine from his nightstand and prayed out loud, "Dear God, help me kill this spider! Don't let me miss!"

He whacked the spider and it fell to the floor.

"I'll throw it out the window," Michael said. He slid the magazine carefully under the dead spider. Feeling brave now that the spider was dead, he bent over to take a closer look. Then he caught his breath and gave a low whistle.

"Mom, look! This isn't an ordinary spider! See the red hourglass marking on its belly? This is a black widow—it's poisonous!"

Shivers ran down Michael's arms. His new-found bravery melted. "If there's one spider, there must be more," he whispered. "Oh, Mom! I can't stand the thought of more spiders. What if they have a nest in the basement? What if they bite the baby?"

Mother drew a deep breath and said, "I know God provided this home for us. All we can do is ask him to care for us. Let's pray." And Mother knelt down with Michael.

Michael began, "Thank you, God, for giving me courage to kill the spider. Thanks for not letting it bite any of us. Please make all other black widow spiders come out in the open so we can get rid of them. And Lord, help me be brave about this."

Later Michael told their pastor, "God answered our prayers! One by one we found the spiders. Every time we saw one, God gave us the courage to kill it. Finally there were no more black widows. And best of all, somehow God took away our fear of spiders."

What About You?

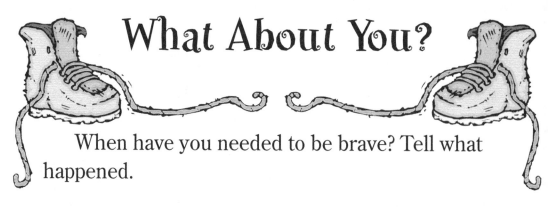

When have you needed to be brave? Tell what happened.

What things make you feel afraid?

What helps you keep trying and not give up?

You may need courage to play a new sport you've never played or to get back on your bike after you've crashed. You need to be brave when you move to a new neighborhood or attend a different school.

Long ago the Israelites were afraid of their neighbors. The Midianite army destroyed their crops, their land, and all their animals. The Israelites were helpless against the huge army. Finally they cried out to God for help.

God sent an angel to a young man named Gideon who was hiding from the enemies. God told Gideon, "Go and save Israel. I am sending you."

But Gideon was afraid of the huge enemy army. He didn't think he could lead an army to fight against them. Find out what helped Gideon to be brave.

God Helped Gideon and Purah to Be Brave
Judges 7:1-22

As the enemy was preparing to attack, God told Gideon, "You will win this battle. But you have too many men. They will brag that they saved Israel with their own strength. I will save Israel with the help of only three hundred men. Send all the others home." So Gideon did.

That night God told Gideon, "Get up. I will help you win this battle. If you are afraid to attack, take your servant Purah with you and go secretly to the enemy's camp. Listen to what they say. Then you will not be afraid to fight their army."

Gideon and Purah crept down the mountain to the edge of the camp. They overheard a man inside the tent telling his dream to a friend.

The friend said, "Your dream means that God will hand our army over to Gideon and the Israelite army!"

When Gideon heard this, he rejoiced and he worshiped God. He was no longer afraid. Returning to camp, he awakened his men and told them the good news.

Gideon separated the three hundred men into three groups. He gave each man a trumpet and an empty jar with a torch inside.

Gideon said, "Do what I do. We'll blow our trumpets, break the jars, and shout the battle cry: 'For God and for Gideon!'"

When Gideon's army blew the trumpets, God caused all the enemy soldiers to fight each other!

More than a hundred and twenty thousand of the Midianite soldiers died in battle that day. The fifteen thousand soldiers who were still alive ran away as far and as fast as they could. But Gideon and his little army chased after them and destroyed them all.

Now God brought peace to the land of Israel. God had made one fearful man into a brave leader. And afterward Gideon became the ruler over all of Israel.

What Does This Mean for You?

To Think About

- God has often used frightened people to do big jobs. Has there been a time when God made you brave so you could do a very hard job?

- How did you feel?

- What if God gave you a big job to do? Would you be brave and courageous?

ALWAYS REMEMBER

- Whenever you feel frightened, ask God for strength to be brave. God will help you to be courageous like Michael and Gideon.

- Nothing is too hard for God. God can always give you strength to face the impossible. Trust God to give you courage. Then give God the credit for every victory!

- God doesn't promise to take away all your fears and problems. God has promised to make you strong and brave so you can face your fears and conquer them.

GOD'S TREASURY OF PROMISES

Be strong and take heart, all you who hope in the Lord.
Psalm 31:24

The Lord gives strength to his people.
Psalm 29:11

The Lord is my light and my salvation—whom shall I fear?
The Lord is the stronghold of my life—of whom shall
I be afraid?
Psalm 27:1

I can do everything through God who gives me strength.
Philippians 4:13

Be strong and very courageous. Be careful to obey all the
law . . . that you may be successful wherever you go.
Joshua 1:7

Chapter 5

God's Promise:
I Will Lead You
and Guide You

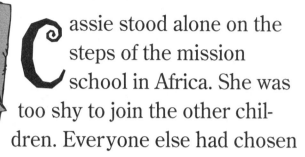

Cassie stood alone on the steps of the mission school in Africa. She was too shy to join the other children. Everyone else had chosen a partner. No one had chosen Cassie.

"All right, let's go," called the schoolmaster to the students. "We need to be back in time for supper. Stick together and follow our guide. I don't want anybody to go off the path and get lost! It would be hard to find you in this tall grass."

Cassie tagged along behind the row of partners. With every step she took, her stomach ached more and more. Tears filled her eyes as she watched everyone else laughing and talking together.

It was hard to be in this boarding school for children whose parents are missionaries in Africa. It was hard for Cassie to leave her mother and father and little sister.

Dear God, I know you led my parents to be missionaries here in Africa. And I know you brought me to this school. Help me be happy here.

"Stay together," the schoolmaster shouted down the line of children.

Hiking through the waist-high grass, Cassie struggled to keep up with the bigger kids. The grass was so tall that it sometimes pricked her chin and scratched her neck.

Suddenly a huge butterfly the size of a hand flew past her, weaving among the nearby flowering bushes. Cassie forgot everything else. Bending low in the grass, she followed the fluttering insect. Finally it came to rest on a bright yellow flower. She quietly crept within a foot of the beautiful butterfly. In awe she watched it feed while it gently fanned its wings.

When the butterfly finished snacking, it flapped its wings and flew up high in the air.

Then Cassie remembered—*I'm supposed to stay with the group. But where did they go? And where is the trail?*

Cassie climbed on a rock and looked in every direction above the tall grass. She tried to gather her thoughts.

Did they go up into the foothills? Or walk to the grove of trees up ahead? Oh, how can I find my way without the leader? I don't even know what direction I came from!

Heart pounding, she prayed aloud, "Dear God, it's just you and me now. Please be my leader. Help me know what to do and where to go."

Just then a thought popped into Cassie's mind: *If I try to find the others, I may end up even farther from school. And they may have a harder time finding me. But if I go back the way we came, God will help me find my way to the school.*

And that's what Cassie did. It wasn't too hard to follow the trail in the grass that had been crushed by the children as they walked. Soon she arrived back at the school.

That night at dinner at the school, Cassie's teacher sat down next to her. "Cassie? We were worried sick about you."

Cassie explained to her teacher and the others, "I couldn't keep up and I couldn't see the leader. I called but you didn't hear me. So I asked God to lead me. And he did. He gave me the thought that I should not try to go on, but I should try to find my way back. God helped me stay calm. I was really frightened, but I didn't even cry," she added softly.

The other children knew how easy—and how scary—it was to get lost. They all cheered for Cassie!

Cassie smiled and looked all around the room. These kids and the teacher had really been worried about her. *They do like me,* thought Cassie.

Finally Cassie didn't feel alone anymore. Now she felt at home.

What About You?

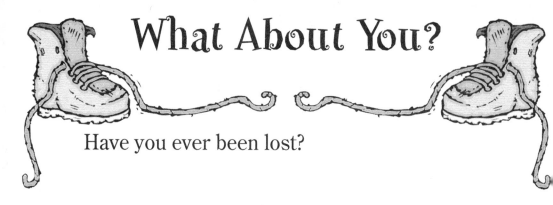

Have you ever been lost?

It's scary! How did you feel?

Did you ever wonder what to do next?

Maybe you've been in the car with your parents when they got lost. Did they stop to ask directions?

When you are lost, you desperately need good *directions.* You find God's directions in his Word, the Bible. The Bible is like a light that shows you who God is, who you are, and what God wants you to do.

God's Word will help you make the right choices when you need directions.

God Led Abraham's Servant
Genesis 24

Abraham knew he didn't have long to live.
Now he was concerned about his only son, Isaac.
He did not want his son to take a wife from the
people who lived around him. None of them
believed in the Lord God.

So Abraham called his servant and said, "The
Lord is the God of heaven and the God of earth. I
want you to promise me that you won't get a wife
for my son from the people of this land. Go to the
country I came from many years ago and find a
young girl from among my relatives to marry
Isaac."

The servant promised to do what his master
asked. He loaded ten camels with many expensive gifts and started the long journey to the town
where Abraham's relatives lived.

When the servant arrived at a well outside of
town, it was time for the women to come out to

get water. He wondered how he would know which girl would be the right one for Isaac.

He prayed, "Lord, help me know the right girl. When I ask her for a drink, let her offer to water all my camels." (Ten thirsty camels can drink a *lot* of water!)

Before he had finished praying, a girl named Rebekah walked toward the well. The servant asked for a drink of water from her jar.

She smiled and poured him a drink. Then she offered, "I'll water your camels, too." She went back and forth to the well many times until the camels finished drinking.

"Whose daughter are you?" asked the servant.

She answered, "I am Rebekah. I'm the daughter of Bethuel and the granddaughter of Nahor."

The servant gasped! Nahor was Abraham's brother! The servant bowed and worshiped God for answering his prayer!

When the servant brought Rebekah back to Isaac, he told Isaac how the Lord had led and guided him. Isaac married Rebekah and loved her.

What Does This Mean for You?

To Think About

- When has God helped you know what to do or where to go?

- How did you find your way?

- What are some ways in which God leads you each day?

- What would you do if you were lost and needed directions?

ALWAYS REMEMBER

- Whenever you wonder what to do, you can ask God to lead you. God has promised to help you make the right choices and decisions.

- God knows everything. God knows when you feel confused and don't know what to do or where to go. God wants you to come to him for directions.

- God uses the Bible as well as other people to teach you his ways, to make you wise, and to lead and guide you each day of your life.

GOD'S TREASURY OF PROMISES

God said, "I will instruct you and teach you
in the way you should go."
Psalm 32:8

Your hand will guide me, O Lord.
Psalm 139:10

Your word, O God, is a lamp to my feet and a light for my path.
Psalm 119:105

This God is our God for ever and ever;
he will be our guide even to the end.
Psalm 48:14

Whether you turn to the right or to the left,
your ears will hear God's voice behind you, saying,
"This is the way; walk in it."
Isaiah 30:21

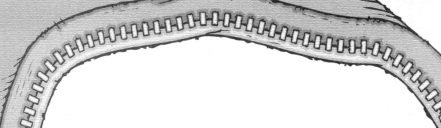

Chapter 6

God's Promise:
I Will Send
My Angels to
Guard You

D ad turned to twelve-year-old Emery and patted him on the shoulder. "Do you think you can manage these kids for about an hour while I drive Mom over to Grandma's house?"

"Sure, Dad," Emery told him. "I know Grandma's really sick and needs Mom to help her. Don't worry about us. I can take care of all the little kids."

The kids stood in the doorway and waved good-bye to their parents. Then Emery said to his four younger brothers and sisters, "Come inside. Get your pajamas on, and I'll fix you a snack before you go to bed."

The four little kids hurried inside and ran upstairs to change into their pajamas.

While Emery washed some grapes and opened a box of graham crackers, he thought about his grandma. She had been unable to get out of bed since her heart attack. Now she also had a high fever. He was concerned about her. The least he could do was take care of the kids for an hour until Dad got back.

Glancing at the clock, Emery tried to plan what he would do next to get the little ones to settle down and get ready to sleep.

As he set out the crackers and grapes, he thought, *They'll quiet down faster in the candlelight.* He found a box of matches and lit two candles and placed them on the table. Then he turned off the overhead light.

The four youngsters' eyes sparkled with reflections from the flames as they scurried into the kitchen and sat down around the table.

"I'll read a Bible story while you eat your snack," said Emery. He sat in the rocking chair and began to read.

Halfway through the story, Emery heard five-year-old Kate whisper, "Uh-oh!"

Glancing up, Emery saw three-year-old Jordan lift a fistful of matches and hold them toward the flame. Suddenly the candle tipped over and the matches burst into flames!

Everyone screamed. Jordan threw the matches on the table, catching the tablecloth on fire.

Emery leaped out of the chair, his heart pounding. *Why didn't I put the matches away? Why did I think it was a good idea to light candles? I should have known better,* he thought. He rushed to the sink, grabbed a pitcher, and began to fill it with water. Looking back, he saw the flames spreading across the table toward Kate. She sat frozen, too scared to move.

Suddenly Emery felt that someone was standing behind him! Chills ran down his neck and arms. He quickly turned toward the kitchen door.

There in the doorway stood a tall, beautiful angel. Emery blinked his eyes. *Am I seeing things?* He looked at the other children. All of them were staring wide-eyed at the doorway, too.

For just a few moments as he gazed at the bright angel, he forgot the fire. Then when he finally looked back, flames covered the entire length of the table!

Frantically he turned again to the angel. Emery stared in amazement as the powerful angel took a very deep breath and blew a stream of air toward the blaze.

The roaring flames instantly shriveled to nothing! Only a tiny wisp of smoke remained. The children gasped! Emery stood with his mouth hanging open.

Then the angel just disappeared.

For a moment no one spoke. Then Kate whispered, "Was it . . . was it . . . God's angel?"

Emery nodded. Very quietly the children tiptoed upstairs. Before climbing into bed, they knelt down, said their prayers, and thanked God for his angel.

Emery had quite a story to tell when his dad returned a few minutes later. He admitted his foolish mistake of lighting candles and described the fire and the rescue by an angel. Many years later when the children were grown and had their own families, they still talked about the angel who had rescued them.

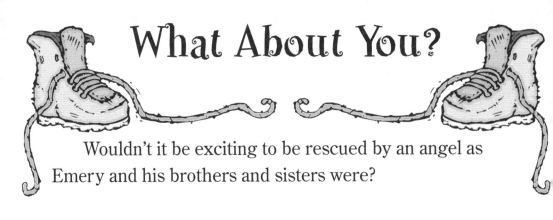

What About You?

Wouldn't it be exciting to be rescued by an angel as Emery and his brothers and sisters were?

Have you ever wished you could see one of God's angels?

Most of us won't get to see an angel until we get to heaven. But we can still be sure that angels are at work in our lives. God has promised to send angels to guard us. We probably don't know how many times angels have kept us from harm or danger.

Someday in heaven God may show you all the times angels protected and helped you. And you will be amazed!

Sometimes God's angels have warned people of danger. Angels warned Joseph, the earthly father of Jesus, to leave the country of Israel and get away from an evil king.

At other times angels have protected people like Daniel in the lions' den and the three young men who were thrown into a fiery furnace.

Now let's read in the Bible about a time when God's angel rescued one of Jesus' disciples just before King Herod was going to have him killed.

God's Angel Rescued Peter
Acts 12:1-19

King Herod hated the apostles of the early Christian church. He made plans to stop them from preaching about Jesus' death and resurrection.

One day King Herod had the apostle James killed with a sword. When Herod found out that many of the Jewish leaders were happy with the death of James, he also arrested Peter and planned to kill him, too.

The king decided that first he would have Peter put on public trial and then have him executed. Since this was the time of the most important Jewish holiday— Passover Feast—the trial and execution were postponed for a few days.

In prison, sixteen soldiers stood guard over Peter. Four soldiers at a time watched him day and night. They even chained Peter between two of them, so there was no chance of escape.

On the night before Herod was going to execute him, Peter was asleep while chained to two soldiers. Two other soldiers guarded his cell door. Other soldiers stood guard in the jail and at the entrance. They wanted to make sure no one would try to rescue Peter.

At the same time, many Christians met together to pray all night for Peter. They knew the king was going to kill him the next day.

Suddenly an angel of the Lord appeared in Peter's cell. Peter woke up as the angel struck him on his side. He put up his hand to shield his eyes from the bright light.

"Quick!" the angel said. "Get up!"

Peter stood up, as the angel directed. The chains fell off his wrists. All four guards went on sleeping.

"Put on your clothes and sandals," said the angel. "And put on your coat. Then follow me."

The angel opened the locked door of Peter's cell. Peter followed closely as the angel led him through the prison. Peter couldn't believe it was really happening! He couldn't believe he was being freed.

Peter and the angel walked past the first guards and the second guards. When they came to the iron gate that led to the city street, it opened by itself and they walked through it.

In a daze, Peter followed the angel down the street. Then the angel disappeared.

Peter realized he was free! He ran to the house where many people were praying for him. There he shared the story of how God's angel had rescued him.

He said, "I know for sure that God sent his angel. He rescued me and set me free from Herod's power. He saved me from a certain death."

What Does This Mean for You?

To Think About

- How does God's promise of angel helpers make you feel?

- Does it help you feel less worried?

- Has there been a time when you wondered if an angel helped you?

- What happened?

- Are you willing to trust that God's angels are with you, even if you never see an angel here on earth?

ALWAYS REMEMBER

- God's invisible angel helpers are always with you—even when you can't see them. Someday you will see them in heaven.

- Angels did not rescue Jesus from the cross. But God sent an angel to strengthen Jesus. Angels did not stop Daniel from being thrown into the lions' den. But an angel went into the lions' den with Daniel.

- God never promised that angels would keep you from ever being hurt or having trouble. But they guard and watch over you, even during times of pain and trouble.

GOD'S TREASURY OF PROMISES

Are not all angels ministering spirits sent to serve
those who will inherit salvation?
Hebrews 1:14

The angel of the Lord encamps around those
who fear him, and he delivers them.
Psalm 34:7

God will command his angels concerning you to guard you
in all your ways; they will lift you up in their hands,
so that you will not strike your foot against a stone.
Psalm 91:11–12

Jesus said, "See that you do not look down on one of these
little ones. For I tell you that their angels in heaven always see
the face of my Father in heaven."
Matthew 18:10

Do not forget to entertain strangers, for by so doing some
people have entertained angels without knowing it.
Hebrews 13:2

Chapter 7

God's Promise:
I Will Answer
Your Prayers

O h!" gasped Lindsay's mother. She jerked the steering wheel to the right and drove the car onto the gravel at the edge of the road and stopped.

Eight-year-old Lindsay's heart pounded. *Is Mom having a heart attack?* She reached over and took hold of her mother's arm. "Mom! What's the matter? Are you okay?" She could feel her mother's arm trembling.

Mother leaned forward, rested her head against the steering wheel, and whispered, "I'm all right, honey. Something amazing just happened."

"What?" asked Lindsay.

"I just felt the presence of the Lord all around me," said Mother softly. "The Lord called my name. I heard him say very clearly, 'There is another child in Korea. It is very important that you bring her to your home.'"

Lindsay thought about their family of seven. Her mother had two daughters. Then Mother and Father had adopted a baby girl and two more little girls, one who was from Korea, but who did not speak Korean.

"But Mom, we already have a full house. Are you sure God is telling you to adopt another child … another *girl?*"

Later Lindsay's father listened quietly as his wife explained to the whole family what had happened that day. He was silent for a moment. Then he reached out to hug his wife and all five daughters. "Of course we'll bring her here. She must be a very special child for God to speak to you like that!"

Lindsay's parents phoned the Holt Adoption Agency in Oregon and applied to adopt a girl from Korea.

When the news came back that they would receive a ten-year-old girl, Lindsay wondered what her new sister, Cammi, would be like. She fixed up her bedroom and put a colorful patchwork quilt on the other twin bed where her new sister would sleep.

Finally the big day came, and the whole family went to the airport to get Cammi.

"How will we talk to her if she doesn't speak English?" Lindsay asked her parents.

"Let's ask the Lord to help us," Father said. The family joined hands and prayed that God would help them find a way to talk to Cammi. Within just a few minutes an older man came up and asked, "Are you waiting for the plane from Korea?"

"Yes. We're here to meet our adopted daughter," explained Mother.

"Oh, how wonderful! May I help you? I speak the Korean language," the man said.

"Oh, yes! It would help if you could tell her about us and let her know that we love her."

When Cammi arrived, the gentleman stepped forward and greeted her in Korean. He told her about her new family and pointed to each of them as he talked. Then he introduced each one.

Everyone hugged Cammi. Then Lindsay turned to thank the man who had helped them, but he was gone.

In her new home, Cammi cheerfully helped everyone. She had lived in an orphanage all her life, where she grew up taking care of the littler children. So she took excellent care of the baby and the two little girls. But it was hard to talk to Cammi because she didn't speak English. The family wished they could say more to her. Finally she began to learn a little English, and finally she could tell them her story.

She said, "American soldiers would bring us food and toys. But more than anything, I wanted a mama and daddy in America.

"I asked the workers at the orphanage if this were possible. But they all told me, 'No. Americans will not want you. You look too different from them.'

"After that I stopped asking the workers. But every night I knelt by my mat and prayed to God."

Lindsay smiled. While Cammi prayed and waited in Korea, God worked to answer her prayers. He spoke to her mother out on the highway and made her heart ready to receive another daughter.

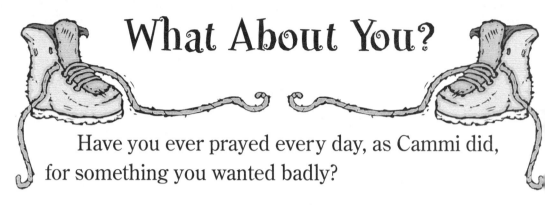

What About You?

Have you ever prayed every day, as Cammi did, for something you wanted badly?

Is there something you have prayed about for a long time?

Have you gotten discouraged and given up praying when it seemed God was not answering?

Stop and think about a time when you had to wait for your mother to help you. Maybe she was slow. But just because you didn't get an answer right away didn't mean your mother didn't love you or wouldn't help you as soon as she could.

Can you remember some people in the Bible who prayed to God and did not get an answer right away?

God Answered Elijah's Prayer
1 Kings 18:41-46

Elijah was a great man of prayer. He wanted to show people that the Lord was the true God. So he had a contest on Mount Carmel with prophets of Baal.

The prophets of Baal prayed for hours. They shouted and cut themselves, begging Baal to answer their prayers.

Then Elijah prayed one short, simple prayer. He asked God to show himself as the one true God. Immediately fire fell from heaven and burned up the sacrificial bull. It even burned up the stone altar!

Right after God sent a mighty fire in answer to Elijah's prayer on the mountain, Elijah met with King Ahab. It had not rained for three years in the land of Israel. Everything was dry. All the plants had died. Nothing would grow anymore. The king was worried.

Elijah told the king, "Go and eat. I know God will send a heavy rain soon. The time of famine will end."

Elijah prayed and then said to his servant, "I know God will send rain. Go and look toward the sea. Watch for a cloud."

So the servant went and looked out over the calm water of the Mediterranean Sea.

"I don't see anything in the sky," he told Elijah.

Elijah prayed again and told his servant, "Look once more. Can you see any clouds?"

"No. The sky is clear," said the servant.

But the seventh time Elijah prayed, his servant reported, "I see a cloud! It's small—about the size of a man's hand. It's coming up over the horizon at the edge of the sea."

Elijah jumped up. "Go to Ahab. Tell him to tie his chariot to his horse and hurry down the mountain before the rain comes!"

Black clouds filled the sky, the wind came up, and the rain began to fall. Elijah ran as fast as he could. He even raced Ahab riding in his chariot, and by God's spirit helping him Elijah won!

What Does This Mean for You?

To Think About

- When has God answered one of your prayers? Tell what happened.

- How did you feel?

- Have you ever felt that God did not answer your prayers?

- Has God ever responded to your prayer with an answer of no?

- Were you disappointed?

- Did the disappointment keep you from trusting God? Why or why not?

ALWAYS REMEMBER

- God hears every whisper and all the thoughts in your head. Don't give up praying, even when you have to wait for an answer.

- God knows everything. So God knows how best to answer your prayers. Don't be discouraged if your prayers aren't answered right away. Wait patiently.

- God may answer you by saying, "Yes," "No," or "Wait," just as your parents sometimes say. God loves to say yes when something is good for you.

GOD'S TREASURY OF PROMISES

Ask and you will receive, and your joy will be complete.
John 16:24

Ask and it will be given to you. . . . For everyone who asks receives.
Matthew 7:7—8

I want men everywhere to lift up holy hands in prayer, without anger or disputing.
1 Timothy 2:8

Jesus said, "If you remain in me and my words remain in you, ask whatever you wish, and it will be given you."
John 15:7

I urge . . . first of all, that requests, prayers, intercession and thanksgiving be made for everyone.
1 Timothy 2:1

Chapter 8

God's Promise: I Will Help You in Times of Trouble

Seven-year-old Eric anxiously tugged his mother's sleeve as she shopped in the grocery store.

"Hurry up, Mom. We need to go home soon. It's getting dark. It's a long way, and I forgot to bring the flashlight."

Since their car was being repaired, Mother had walked to the grocery store. Eric had come along to help carry the groceries back home. It was a half-hour walk from the store to their home just outside of town.

It always takes Mom so long to shop! thought Eric. *I wish she'd hurry.*

Mother picked up a loaf of bread, several cans of soup, and a couple of cans of tuna. When Eric saw her reach for a large canned ham, he reminded her, "Mom, we'll have to carry that!" But she ignored him and added it to the cart anyway.

Eric filled a small paper bag with apples while his mother picked out some oranges. Finally they headed to the checkout stand.

Pushing the cart down the aisle, Eric stumbled. *These stupid shoelaces! They always come untied!*

He stooped down and retied the strings, adding an extra knot to make sure they stayed tied.

When they stepped out of the store, Mother caught her breath. "Oh! It's late," she said. "It won't be light much longer. Let's take the shortcut home across the railroad tracks."

When they reached the tracks, Eric looked up and down the rails. "I hope the evening train has already come and gone," he said. Then just as Eric stepped over the side rail, he tripped and lost his balance.

His foot slid sideways and wedged in a hole between two wooden planks. Apples spilled everywhere as he tumbled to the ground.

"Are you hurt?" asked Mother as she started scooping up the fruit.

"No," said Eric. "I'll be fine." But when he tried to get up, his foot was stuck tight.

Mother bent down to look. "Untie your shoe and pull out your foot. Then we'll pull out your shoe."

"Oh no!" cried Eric. "I just tied those shoelaces with a double knot!" He struggled to loosen the laces. "I can't untie it, Mom. Can you?"

Then they heard it—a humming noise vibrated from the steel rails. Eric's heart pounded. The train was coming!

Mother tried yanking Eric's foot out of the shoe, but the laces were too tight. She tugged at the knot but couldn't get it loose.

Eric glanced down the tracks and saw the train's light in the distance. Now he panicked.

"God, help us!" Eric prayed out loud. "Help Mom get my shoe off!"

Just as Eric finished praying, Mother's eyes opened wide. "The ham!" she shouted.

Reaching into her bag of groceries, she pulled out the can of ham. She twisted off the small key and peeled open the metal lid.

Using the sharp edge of the lid, Mom cut the knot. Quickly she loosened the laces and yanked

Eric's foot out of the shoe. The train's warning whistle blasted in their ears. It was very close. She grabbed Eric and dragged him over the rails.

As they tumbled down the rocky slope, the train roared past. For a few minutes they just lay on the gravel, shaking so hard they couldn't get up.

Finally Eric said, "Whew! Oh, Mom—I know God answered my prayer and put that idea about the can of ham in your head. But that was way too close."

"You're not kidding about that," Mom said. She slowly stood up, brushed the dirt from her clothing, and picked up the spilled groceries.

"Guess we'd better go on home, Eric," Mom said.

Eric nodded. By now it was completely dark, but he was no longer nervous about the darkness. He knew that the God who had saved them from the train would be with them and help them through any trouble.

What About You?

Wow! Eric had some scary trouble, didn't he? Have you ever been in trouble that serious?

What happened to you then?

When you were in trouble, what did you want to do? Run and hide? Get as far away from the trouble as you could?

Maybe you have a secret hiding place—a spot where you watch for trouble but no one sees you or bothers you.

Do you feel safe when you hide there?

What helps you the most during times of trouble?

Once there was a young man who had been chosen by God to be king. Now, you'd think life would be pretty easy for some-body who had been chosen as the next king of his land, wouldn't you? But oh, no. This young man was in big trouble. He *really* needed a hiding place. He *really* needed God's help! He was being chased by a jealous madman who wanted to kill him.

So if you want to learn who he was and how God keeps his promise to help anyone who is in trouble, read on.

God Helped David in a Time of Trouble
1 Samuel 24:2-22

Long ago a teenager named David killed Goliath the giant warrior. The people cheered for David. He was their hero. Saul, the king of Israel, felt jealous and decided to get rid of him.

When David heard about the king's plans, he ran to the mountains. His brothers and six hundred other men who wanted David to be their leader followed him.

King Saul took three thousand of his best soldiers and went to find him. With that many after him, David knew he desperately needed to find a safe place. So he prayed, "I trust in you, Lord. You are my God.... Save me from my enemies. Save me from those who are chasing me." And God showed David a good hiding place—a cave.

Finally the king and his men arrived at the cave where David and his men were hiding. King Saul went into the cave to rest.

Crouched behind the rocks, David's men whispered to him, "Here's your chance. Go kill him!" David refused. Instead he quietly crept close to Saul and cut off a corner of the king's robe.

In the morning David waited until Saul left the cave. Then David went out of the cave and called, "King Saul!"

First David bowed to Saul to show his respect. Then, holding up the piece of Saul's robe, David said, "See how close I was to you in the cave? My men begged me to kill you, but I wouldn't. I do not wish to harm you."

Then he said, "May God show you that I'm not guilty of doing anything wrong. And may God save me from being destroyed by your powerful hand."

Weeping out loud, Saul told David, "May God reward you for the way you treated me today. You are a better person than I am." And he went back home to his palace. God had answered David's prayer.

What Does This Mean for You?

To Think About

- What troubles have you experienced in your life?

- When has God protected you from danger?

- What is the worst thing that ever happened to you?

- What were some ways in which God helped you during that time?

ALWAYS REMEMBER

- Sometimes God stops bad things from happening. But sometimes God *allows* problems and troubles to come. During hard times, God is still with you.

- Everyone has troubles. Jesus told his disciples, "In this world you will have trouble. But take heart! I have overcome the world" (John 16:33). Don't let your troubles keep you from trusting Jesus and being happy in him.

- God is always ready to help you. During times of trouble, God will help you know what to do or where to go, just as he helped Eric and young David.

GOD'S TREASURY OF PROMISES

My shield is God Most High, who saves the upright in heart.
Psalm 7:10

God says, "Call upon me in the day of trouble;
I will deliver you, and you will honor me."
Psalm 50:15

The Lord is faithful, and he will strengthen
and protect you from the evil one.
2 Thessalonians 3:3

God is our refuge and strength,
an ever-present help in trouble.
Psalm 46:1

A righteous man may have many troubles,
but the Lord delivers him from them all.
Psalm 34:19

Chapter 9

God's Promise:
I Will Save You

E asy there, Henny," Devon talked in a low voice to her pet chicken. "Are your eggs finally ready to hatch?" Devon poked in the hay lining the hen's nest.

Henny kept a close eye on Devon. She was protective of her eggs. Usually she pecked anyone who came near her nest and especially those who tried to poke around under her. Everyone, that is, except Devon.

Then Devon heard a new sound above Henny's quiet clucking! There were tiny peeps.

"Henny! Your babies are hatching!"

Devon watched excitedly as six fluffy yellow heads poked out from underneath their mother.

That week, every afternoon after school, Devon spent time in the barnyard with Henny and the baby chicks. Devon loved to watch the mother hen teaching her little brood to hunt for worms and to watch for the hawks overhead.

One afternoon when Devon arrived home, dark clouds were rolling up on the horizon. She found her father in the barn and asked him, "Dad, the sky looks strange. What's happening down the road?"

Dad ran out of the barn and looked where Devon pointed. He took a deep breath and said quietly, "Uh-oh! It's a prairie fire! We need to work fast. Get the hose!"

The terrible fire burning out of control across the Kansas prairie came closer and closer. It burned everything in its path. Soon it moved directly toward the farmland belonging to Devon's father.

First Dad tried to phone for help. Then he came to find Devon.

"There's no one to help us," he said as he grabbed a shovel and another hose. "They're all trying to save their own farms. Here—keep the grass wet. Put out any sparks that land close to our house."

Devon and her father each took a long hose. They watered all the grass and hay around the house and the barn to keep them from catching on fire.

Someone else on the farm saw the danger, too—Henny! Devon heard Henny call to the baby chicks. She saw the babies come running at the sound of their mother's warning. Henny tucked them underneath her wings to protect them.

All evening and all through the night, Devon helped hose down the sparks that landed close to their house. By morning the fire had burned out and the house was safe. But the fast-moving fire had burned down the barn and destroyed all their cornfields.

At dawn Devon and her father searched the surrounding fields for small fires that were still burning. They hosed down every smoking ember that could erupt into another blaze.

Devon felt exhausted. "I've been working all night, Dad. I need to sleep," she said, heading to the house.

Suddenly she remembered Henny. Her pet chicken was nowhere to be seen. Devon looked in the henhouse. Her pet and her babies weren't there. Where were they? Were they still alive . . . or dead?

"Henny! Where are you?" she called again and again, but there was no answer.

In the charred ruins of the barn, her father pushed over a clump of something that was still burning. Devon reached him just as he pushed it over with the shovel.

To their surprise, six fluffy yellow chicks burst out from beneath the clump!

Devon gathered the chicks in her arms. "Oh, you dear babies! I'm so glad you're alive." Then she paused. "But . . . where is your mother?"

Then she knelt by her dad and tears came to her eyes as she examined the burned clump. It was Henny! Devon held the chicks close. The brave little mother hen had given her life to save her babies.

What About You?

What a gift that mother hen gave to her chicks—the gift of life! It was sad that she had to die. Her greatest gift was love. Why do you think any animal—or any person— would give a life so another could live?

The highest gift of all is a gift of love. Do you love someone enough to give your life for that person? Who?

Would you be willing to give your life for someone who was mean to you or hated you? Why or why not?

Did you know that Jesus said he felt like a mother hen who wanted to protect her chicks?

When he rode to Jerusalem on Palm Sunday, he looked over the city and wept. He knew the city would soon be destroyed. Jesus said, "O Jerusalem, Jerusalem, . . . how often I have longed to gather your children together, as a hen gathers her chicks under her wings, but you were not willing!" (Matthew 23:37).

Read the story of how God loved us and gave his best gift to save us—even when people didn't want to receive his gift.

God Saved All People
Luke 1:26-38; 2:10-12:2

"Greetings, Mary. Don't be afraid," said the angel. "God is very pleased with you. You will give birth to a son. You must name him Jesus. He will be great and will be called the Son of the most high God. He will rule forever. His kingdom will never end."

"I serve the Lord," Mary answered. "May it happen to me just as you said it would."

Mary was about to marry a man named Joseph. When she told him she was going to have a baby—God's own Son—he didn't believe it.

But then an angel of the Lord appeared to Joseph in a dream and said, "Joseph, son of David, don't be afraid to take Mary home to be your wife. The baby inside her is from the Holy Spirit. She will have a son. You are to give him the name Jesus, because he will save his people from their sins."

When Jesus was about thirty years old, he left his home and traveled through the land with his disciples.

Mary and many other people who followed Jesus believed that he was the Son of God and the promised Savior. They rejoiced that God loved them and had sent his Son to save them.

But most people thought Jesus was going to save them from the Romans who ruled their land. They thought he would rule the land of Israel as an *earthly* king. They didn't realize that his kingdom was in heaven.

Then something unexpected happened. A crowd of soldiers and Jewish leaders arrested Jesus. Mary watched as the soldiers nailed Jesus to a cross. She watched as he died. Nobody standing at the cross understood that he was giving his life so that we could live forever as children of God!

On Resurrection Sunday Jesus rose from the dead and appeared to his mother and his other followers. He helped them understand that he loved them and that he had given his life to become their Savior.

Thank God for the greatest gift of love— Jesus!

What Does This Mean for You?

To Think About

- Do you trust and believe that Jesus is your Savior?

- Even if you had been the only person in the whole world who needed a Savior, Jesus would still have given his life to save you. Has there been a time when you wondered if God really loved you?

- Why can you be certain that God loves you and has saved you?

ALWAYS REMEMBER

- God has shown you his love by sending Jesus to die for you. Jesus brings you close to God. Now you are God's child.

- Whenever you wonder if God loves you, just look in the manger. Then look at the cross and the empty grave.

- Nobody receives God's love because they deserve it. No one can ever earn God's love or buy it. It is always a gift. Have you received God's gift of love? If you haven't, take time to do it now.

GOD'S TREASURY OF PROMISES

The angel told Joseph, "You are to give him the name Jesus, because he will save his people from their sins."
Matthew 1:21

God so loved the world that he gave his one and only Son, that whoever believes in him shall not perish but have eternal life.
John 3:16

Jesus said, "Whoever believes and is baptized will be saved."
Mark 16:16

Paul told the jailer, "Believe in the Lord Jesus, and you will be saved—you and your household."
Acts 16:31

It is by grace you have been saved, through faith . . . it is the gift of God.
Ephesians 2:8

Chapter 10

God's Promise: I Will Stay Close to You and Hold Your Hand

CRACK! *SIZZLE!* BA~BOOMMM!

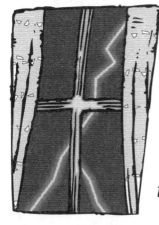

Seven-year-old Derek sat up straight in bed. His whole body shook with fear. *What was that terrible noise?*

Crack! *Sizzle!* A bright flash outside his bedroom window lit up his room for a moment. Then another booming crash shook the house.

"Help!" he yelled right out loud—he couldn't hold back his cry. Cold chills and shivers ran from his head to his toes.

What a storm! It's right on top of our house. I'm not staying upstairs. There's too much lightning and thunder.

Derek threw back his quilt and jumped out of bed. He ran to the window and looked out, wondering what the lightning had hit. He knew it had struck something close by, but he didn't see anything in the backyard.

When Derek opened his bedroom door, he smelled smoke.

Our house must have been hit by the lightning! Something's burning. We've got to get out of here fast!

Derek was still shaking with fear. He wanted to run, but his arms and legs felt as if they were frozen stiff.

"Dear God," he prayed. "Please help me. I'm so scared. Stay with me as I go down these stairs."

Smoke billowed up the stairway to Derek's bedroom. Then Derek remembered what Dad had said.

"Smoke kills more people than fires do. In a fire, get down and crawl. You'll find oxygen close to the ground so you can breathe while you escape."

"Don't leave me, dear God!" prayed Derek as he dropped down on the floor and crawled down the stairway. He hoped his folks had heard the noise and were getting the baby and the twins out safely.

Halfway down the stairs, Derek saw an eerie glow of flickering flames in the living room. It was on fire!

Derek knew he couldn't go out the front door because of the flames. And he didn't think he could get out the back door before the fire and smoke reached the kitchen.

When Derek reached the bottom stair step, he stood up and paused. In the smoky darkness, the only thing he could see was the flicker of spreading flames.

Again he prayed for God's help. Suddenly he felt a warm hand grab his right hand.

"Oh, Daddy! I'm glad you found me. Let's get out of here!" Tears of relief ran down Derek's face as he was led through the darkness.

Derek followed blindly. There was so much smoke that he couldn't see anything in front of him. He did know they were going down the kitchen hallway that led to the back door. He was so glad his father was guiding him.

Finally, after what seemed like years, they went through the kitchen door and outside, where Derek gasped for fresh air.

"Dad . . . we're safe!" Derek waited for his father to speak. "Dad . . . where are you?"

He looked and saw that no one else was around. *Where's Dad?*

As Derek ran around the house to the front yard, he nearly collided with his father!

Father and son hugged each other tightly. Derek felt his father's wet tears against his cheek.

"Derek, you're safe! How did you get out?"

"Of course I'm safe, Dad. You led me outside."

Dad shook his head. "No, I didn't. I brought your mom and the little ones out the front door, but I couldn't get back in because of the flames. And I didn't have any way to open the back door!"

Then Derek knew what happened! "Oh, Dad! I prayed—and God held my hand and led me from the burning house."

What About You?

What a midnight rescue! Hopefully, you haven't been caught in a burning house. You may have had other troubles and hard times that were just as serious and just as frightening. What are some of the scary things that have happened in your life?

Have you ever felt God's hand? How can you be sure God is always with you?

It's not easy to trust God during a crisis or when everything is going wrong. Even grown-ups often feel afraid and need to be reassured that God is with them.

The apostle Paul knew what trouble was, and he knew that God was with him. Paul went through many hard times. He was often imprisoned. He suffered terrible beatings. Five times the Jews gave him thirty-nine lashes with a whip. Three times they beat him with sticks. Once he was nearly stoned to death. And he was shipwrecked three times.

Yet Paul never gave up trusting in God to help him. He knew God would stand with him through every trouble.

On the next page read about a time when Paul and other people on a ship were about to drown.

God Was with Paul and the Sailors
Acts 27

The apostle Paul was arrested for teaching
people about Jesus. The Jewish governor put him,
along with some other prisoners, on a boat that was
to sail to Rome, where Paul would have to stand trial.

Paul knew that winter storms were battering the
Mediterranean Sea. So he warned the ship's officers,
"Men, I can see that our trip is going to be dangerous.
The ship and everything in it will be lost. Our own
lives will be in great danger, also."

But the commander ignored what Paul said. He
pulled up the boat's anchor and set sail.

Before long a powerful storm hit the boat. All
that day the ship took a very bad beating. The next
day the crew began to throw the ship's cargo over-
board to try to save the ship.

On the third day they threw the ship's gear over-
board. Now the storm was so terrible that everyone
finally gave up all hope of surviving. They even
stopped eating.

But one night during the worst of the storm, an angel came to Paul and said, "Don't be afraid, Paul. God is with you. You must go on trial in Rome. God in his grace will spare the lives of all those sailing with you."

The next morning Paul told everyone what the angel had said. Paul encouraged the sailors. "Men, be brave. I have faith that God is here and will help us. But we must run the ship onto the beach of an island."

Later Paul urged the men, "Eat some food. You need it to live. And don't worry, not one of you will lose a single hair from your head. Trust God."

Paul took some bread, gave thanks to God, and ate it. The men felt hopeful and they ate some food, too.

The next morning they saw an island. As they sailed toward the beach, the ship ran aground on a sandbar. Waves pounded the back of the ship and broke it to pieces. So all the 276 men on board had to leave the ship. They either swam or hung on to pieces of the ship, and everyone made it to shore safely.

It was truly a miracle that no one on the ship was lost, just as God's angel had promised. Paul and all the sailors were greatly relieved that God had stayed with them in the time of their greatest trouble.

What Does This Mean for You?

To Think About

- Most of you probably haven't lived through a ship-wreck! But other bad things have probably happened to you. What are some of the hard times you or your family have experienced?

- What has been the most difficult thing that ever happened to you?

- Was it hard to trust God during that time?

- Has there been a time when you felt that God did *not* help you?

- Talk about what happened and how you felt.

ALWAYS REMEMBER

- God has not left you or forgotten about you during hard times. God never promised to keep all storms from your life. But God does promise to always be with you.

- Whenever you are afraid or facing an emergency, know that you are not alone. Ask God to hold your hand.

- No matter what happens, you can trust that God is close beside you. God is holding your hand ... even when you can't *feel* it.

GOD'S TREASURY OF PROMISES

God said, "I am the Lord, your God, who takes hold of your right hand and says to you, Do not fear; I will help you."
Isaiah 41:13

I have set the LORD always before me. Because he is at my right hand, I will not be shaken.
Psalm 16:8

The LORD says, "Fear not. . . . When you pass through the waters, I will be with you. . . . When you walk through the fire, you will not be burned."
Isaiah 43:1–2

Jesus said, "My sheep listen to my voice. . . . No one can snatch them out of my hand."
John 10:27–28

The Lord is my rock, my fortress and my deliverer. . . . He is my shield.
Psalm 18:2

Chapter II

God's Promise:
I Will Forgive You

Brian whistled for his dog, Theo. "Come on, boy! It's time for a bike ride!"

A big, black Labrador came running and wagging his tail. He followed Brian into the garage.

Suddenly Brian's face paled. His brand-new bike lay on the floor beside Dad's car. Brian groaned as he knelt down beside it.

The front tire was flat, and the handlebars were bent to the side. Some of the shiny red paint had been chipped off the back fender, and the front fender was dented.

"Who did this to my bike?" Tears filled Brian's eyes. He slammed his hand on the bike seat. "Where's Cody—he did this!"

Brian ran to the house and went inside. Using both fists, he pounded on his little brother's bedroom door.

"Cody! Come out!" hollered Brian. He turned the doorknob but it was locked. "Open the door! Tell me what you did to my bike!"

From behind the door Cody screamed, "Help, Dad! Brian's going to beat me up!"

Hearing footsteps, Brian turned to face his father.

"But Dad, you'd be mad, too, if he ruined your brand-new bike. He'd better buy me another one—I don't care if it takes all his money for the next ten years!"

Father persuaded Cody to unlock the door. When Cody opened the door, Brian noticed his red eyes and tear-stained cheeks.

Cody threw himself on his bed and sobbed. "I'm sorry. I didn't know how to use the brakes."

Dad sat down beside Cody. "Brian, I want to talk to Cody," Dad said quietly. "Could you please leave us alone for a while?"

Brian stomped outside to the garage. As he turned the doorknob, he heard a muffled yelp.

Oops! When I ran in the house, I must have slammed this door and left Theo in the garage, Brian thought. He opened the door, and the big dog leaped up and knocked him over. Brian rolled in the grass and played with his pet.

But when Brian went back into the garage, he glanced at his dad's new car.

Brian gasped! The doors were both dented. Long claw marks ran down each one. *Oh, no— Theo!*

A stern voice behind Brian asked, "Who's to blame for this damage on my car?"

Brian knew it was his fault. He had been so mad about his bike that he forgot about Theo.

"Who left Theo alone in the garage?" asked Dad.

Brian's heart sank. This was the first *new* car his dad ever owned. He remembered how mad Dad got when he touched the shiny paint and left fingerprints on it. Brian cringed and waited for the tongue-lashing he knew he deserved.

But instead of yelling, Dad put his arm around Brian. "I guess I've been acting too proud of this car. It will wear out someday. You're more valuable to me than any hunk of metal."

Brian sighed with relief. "It's my fault, Dad. Please forgive me. I didn't want your car to get scratched up."

"I forgive you, Son." Dad paused. "And I think someone else may need forgiveness, too."

Brian looked over at Cody standing nearby. He ran and threw his arms around his little brother. "Please forgive me, Cody. I should have been willing to share my bike."

Cody hugged him back. "Forgive me, too. I never wanted to hurt your bike."

Brian looked into Cody's eyes. "You're more important than a little pile of metal. I forgive you."

And Brian smiled as he thought, *What would we do without forgiveness?*

What About You?

It's not easy to forgive, is it? Have you ever felt angry, as Brian did?

What has been the most difficult thing for you to forgive?

Could you finally forgive the person who hurt you? What helped you forgive?

It may take a while to trust someone or be friends again after they've hurt you. You may still *remember* how someone has hurt you, but once you've forgiven someone, do not bring it up again.

Remember—the more you receive forgiveness from God, the more you will be able to forgive others.

Once Peter came to Jesus and asked, "Lord, how many times should I forgive my brother when he sins against me? Shall I forgive him up to seven times?"

Jesus answered, "I tell you, not seven times. You must forgive seventy-seven times."

How do you think Peter felt when he heard that? He was probably shocked! Seventy-seven times seemed like far too many times to forgive someone who hurt you.

So Jesus told the following story to help Peter understand forgiveness.

The Servant Who Wouldn't Forgive
Matthew 18:23-35

Once there was a king who wanted to collect all the money his servants owed him. A servant was brought in who owed the king a lot of money—millions of dollars!

The servant did not have money to pay back the king. So the king ordered that he, his children, his wife, and all he owned should be sold to pay the debt.

The servant fell on his knees in front of the king. "Please, give me time," he begged. "And I'll pay you back everything."

The king felt sorry for his servant. He had mercy on him and forgave him all the debt.

The servant was excited to be free from the terrible debt. But instead of being generous to others, he went and found another servant who owed him a very small debt—only a few dollars.

He grabbed that servant by the throat and yelled, "Pay back what you owe me—now!"

The other servant fell on his knees and begged, "Give me time. I'll pay you back."

But the first servant showed no mercy to the man. He had him thrown in prison. He gave orders to keep the servant in prison until he paid everything he owed.

When other servants saw what he had done, they knew it was not fair. So they told the king everything that had happened.

Then the king called the first servant to come and see him. "You evil servant," said the king. "I forgave you the huge debt you owed me, because you begged me to. Why didn't you show mercy to your fellow servant just as I showed mercy to you?"

The angry king turned him over to the jailers and said, "Punish this wicked servant until he pays back everything he owes."

The message is that God will forgive those who forgive others from the bottom of their hearts.

What Does This Mean for You?

To Think About

- How are you like the servant who owed the king a great debt?

- When do you ask God to forgive you?

- What did it cost God to forgive you?

- Was it easy for Jesus to die on the cross?

- Why did Jesus pay for all you have done wrong?

- Have you forgiven everyone who has hurt you?

- Stop and think if there is someone you need to forgive. If you don't forgive others, can you expect God to forgive you?

ALWAYS REMEMBER

- All through your life, you will need to forgive other people. Don't hold things against other people. Remember how Jesus forgave those who crucified him.

- All through your life, you will need to ask God's forgiveness. Whenever you do something wrong, confess it to God and ask his forgiveness. Then be glad! God forgives you completely.

- Nobody receives God's forgiveness because they deserve it! It is a gift Jesus gives you. He died so you could be forgiven. Now it is up to you to share that same forgiveness with those who hurt you.

GOD'S TREASURY OF PROMISES

Be kind and compassionate to one another, forgiving each other, just as in Christ God forgave you.
Ephesians 4:32

Bear with each other and forgive whatever grievances you may have against one another.
Forgive as the Lord forgave you.
Colossians 3:13

When they hurled their insults at Jesus, he did not retaliate.
1 Peter 2:23

If we confess our sins, God is faithful and just and will forgive us our sins and purify us from all unrighteousness.
1 John 1:9

Jesus said, "Love your enemies and pray for those who persecute you, that you may be sons of your Father in heaven."
Matthew 5:44—45

Chapter 12

God's Promise:
I Will Give You
New Life Forever

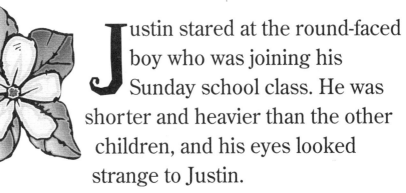

Justin stared at the round-faced boy who was joining his Sunday school class. He was shorter and heavier than the other children, and his eyes looked strange to Justin.

What's wrong with him? wondered Justin.

"Quit staring!" whispered Ryan. "He can't help how he looks. He has Down's syndrome."

"Class," said teacher Gwen, "I want to introduce you to Charlie. He was born with a lot of physical problems. He loves Jesus, and he wants to celebrate Jesus' resurrection with us. Let's give him a warm welcome."

Teacher Gwen led the students in clapping. Charlie laughed as he clapped along with them.

After teacher Gwen told the story of Jesus' death and resurrection, she opened a large box wrapped in silver paper. Reaching inside, she lifted out a decorated basket. It was filled with large plastic eggs of all colors.

"We're going outside today," said teacher Gwen. She handed an egg to each child as she explained,

"God made everything that lives. And Jesus died to give us new life—life that lasts forever.

"Now I want you to look around the church-yard for something that shows 'new life.' When you find it, put it inside your egg and close it shut. Then bring your egg to my basket. When all the eggs have been filled, we'll open them and find out what's inside."

After the children filled their eggs, they put them in the teacher's basket and sat down on the grass to watch her open them.

"Look!" said teacher Gwen, lifting a tiny twig out of a blue egg. "It's a new pussy willow!"

Teacher Gwen opened another egg. "Here's some more new life—a pink bud from another bush."

Other eggs held golden dandelions, tiny white flowers, blades of new green grass, various leaves of different shapes, and a small moth.

When teacher Gwen opened another egg, she frowned. "It's . . . it's empty," she said quietly.

"Someone didn't do it right!" exclaimed Justin. He sat up straight and looked around the group.

Charlie's face turned red. "It's my egg," he said. "And I *did* it . . . I did it right. It's empty . . . just like Jesus' grave!"

Justin quickly put his hand on Charlie's shoulder. "I'm sorry, Charlie, for what I said. You did do it right. The grave was empty. It showed us that Jesus was alive, not dead. I think your egg is the best of all!"

The children clapped their hands and cheered for Charlie, who grinned from ear to ear.

By the end of the month, Charlie was too weak to attend Sunday school. Then one day teacher Gwen told the class, "Charlie died yesterday. We will miss him, but now he's with Jesus."

Justin's eyes filled with tears. He asked, "Can we go to his funeral and do something special for him?"

"Yes," said teacher Gwen. "Anyone who wants to go may sit with me. Let's plan what we can do."

On the day of the funeral, all the children walked to the front of the church together. Justin and teacher Gwen led the way. Instead of bringing flowers, each of the children placed a colored plastic egg on Charlie's casket. The eggs were all empty.

Justin smiled through his tears. He knew that Charlie was already enjoying new life with Jesus.

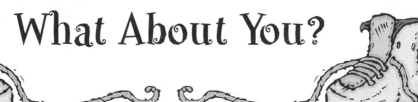

What About You?

Maybe you've had a grandpa or grandma who died. Or perhaps one of your young friends died. How did you feel?

Do you know that everyone cries and feels sad when a loved one dies?

Have you ever worried about what happens after death?

Think about how Jesus' friends and disciples felt when he was crucified. They were very sad.

The disciples were also very scared after Jesus died. But we can't blame them for feeling afraid!

They knew that those who hated Jesus might arrest or even kill them. So they hid behind locked doors.

Do you think any of the disciples believed Jesus would come alive again in a few days?

No, they didn't! They never expected him to rise from the dead. They knew that his body had been buried in the grave and that the stone had been sealed.

God Raised Jesus from the Dead
John 20:1-10, 19-20

"Peter, open the door!" a woman called. "Hurry!"

Peter slowly opened the door. It was Mary. He checked to make sure no one had followed her.

"Shhh. Speak quietly!" he said in a low voice.

"They've taken the Lord!" she said breathlessly. Tears streamed down her face. "It's true! Go and see.... The tomb is empty! I've seen it."

Peter asked Mary, "How could the stone have been moved? What exactly did you see?"

"I went there early this morning to anoint his dead body with spices," Mary said. "The stone had been pushed away from the opening. It would have taken twenty men to push it so far! And Jesus' body is gone!"

Peter frowned. "I'm going there to see for myself!"

He grabbed his cloak and headed out the door. John, the youngest disciple, came, too.

Peter tried to keep up with John as they ran to the tomb, but John ran faster and got there first.

When Peter arrived he rushed past John into the tomb. He could hardly believe his eyes. The mummy-like wrappings still lay tightly wound together.

Where was Jesus' body?

Peter asked John. "How could anyone take the body of Jesus without unwrapping the cloths? Is he alive?"

"Yes," said John quietly. "I think he is."

That evening Jesus suddenly appeared to the disciples and said, "May peace be with you!"

Peter felt terrified. *Is it really Jesus? How did he get through the locked door?*

Jesus held out his hands. Peter stared at the nail marks. It *was* Jesus! His body was new and healed.

Jesus was alive . . . and Peter knew Jesus would never die again!

What Does This Mean for You?

To Think About

- What does it mean to you that Jesus is alive right now?

- How can you be certain that Jesus rose from the dead?

- When you think about a loved one who died, can you trust that they are with Jesus?

- How does that make you feel?

- What are you looking forward to about your new home in heaven?

ALWAYS REMEMBER

- Jesus wants to live with you right now. And he wants you to live with him in heaven. He died and came alive so you could live with him now and forever.

- God is the creator and giver of all life. Take time to look around you for signs of new life in this world. Take time to think about the new life that God has waiting for you in heaven.

- God raised Jesus from the dead. God will also raise to a new life all those who trust Jesus. When someone you love dies, you can be sure you will see them again.

GOD'S TREASURY OF PROMISES

Jesus said, "Because I live, you also will live."
John 14:19

Jesus said, "I am the resurrection and the life. He who believes in me will live, even though he dies."
John 11:25

God who raised Christ from the dead will also give life to your mortal bodies.
Romans 8:11

As in Adam all die, so in Christ all will be made alive.
1 Corinthians 15:22

God has given us eternal life, and this life is in his Son. He who has the Son has life.
1 John 5:11–12

Chapter 13

God's Promise:
I Will Work
Everything Out for
the Best

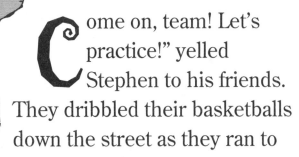

Come on, team! Let's practice!" yelled Stephen to his friends. They dribbled their basketballs down the street as they ran to the empty lot behind the grocery store.

Stephen couldn't believe his eyes! A bulldozer was leveling their homemade basketball court!

"Hey! What are you doing?" Stephen yelled.

He and his friends hollered and waved at the bulldozer operator, trying to make him stop the rig. The man ignored them. He finished bulldozing their court and drove off without a word.

Upset and angry, the boys hurried home.

"What will we do now?" Stephen asked his dad. "Our city tournament starts in two weeks. If we can't practice together, we won't be able to play."

After several phone calls, Stephen's father found out what had happened.

"The owner is trying to clean up the lot behind the grocery store," said Dad. "It was full of old tree stumps and gopher holes. The basketball hoop was all rusty and bent, so they tore it down."

"That didn't bother us when we played," said Stephen. "We've spent a lot of time putting a team together. Now we don't have anyplace to practice. Guess we'll just have to quit."

Dad put his arm around Stephen's shoulder. "Can you trust God to work this out for good?" he asked.

Stephen frowned. "What good could ever come out of this?" He stomped to his room and got ready for bed. But before he fell asleep, he did take time to talk to Jesus about it.

"You know what's happened, Jesus," Stephen prayed. "Help our team stay together. I'll trust you to work this out for good, even though it looks impossible."

A week later Stephen ran through the empty lot on his way home. He stopped, amazed at what he saw!

There lay a new slab of cement—the size of a full basketball court—and four workers were smoothing it out.

Stephen went over to look at it more closely. He asked the men, "What are you doing?"

They smiled. "The owner of this lot wanted to build something good for the neighborhood. He ordered a cement basketball court and two new hoops. You boys will have a great court to play on in about two days!"

Stephen grinned and nodded his head. "Wow, what a surprise! Wait till the team hears about this!"

All the way home, Stephen thanked the Lord.

He prayed, *Thanks, Jesus, for working this out for good. You gave us something a lot better than we had! Thank you for giving our team a chance to play in the tournament.*

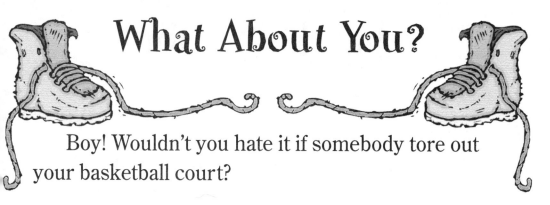

What About You?

Boy! Wouldn't you hate it if somebody tore out your basketball court?

But wouldn't it be fantastic to see a whole new court put in?

How do you respond when something doesn't work out as you planned?

Are you ever shocked when God gives you something so much better than anything you ever asked for or expected?

It is not easy to trust God when things don't work out as we want. Even grown-ups feel upset when things go "wrong."

When has it been hard for you to trust God to work something out for your good?

What About You?

Once a teenager named Joseph went through many troubles. The whole problem started when his father played favorites and loved Joseph more than his other ten sons. He gave Joseph a beautiful coat of many colors. He didn't give coats to any of the other boys. Joseph knew that his ten older brothers were jealous of him.

Then Joseph had a strange dream. Waking up, he ran to tell the dream to his brothers.

"We were tying bundles of wheat in the field. My bundle stood up high, and your bundles bowed to it."

Did his brothers ever get mad! Find out what they did to Joseph—his problems only got *worse!*

God Worked All for Good for Joseph
Genesis 37; 39:1-50:21

One day Joseph told his brothers about a second dream. "The sun, moon, and eleven stars bowed low before me!"

His older brothers laughed. "So you want to be our king, do you? Well, we will *never* bow down to you! *Never!*"

Not long after that, Joseph's brothers grabbed him, ripped off his colorful coat, and threw him down an empty well. Then they sold him as a slave to some foreign traders, who took him to Egypt.

In Egypt Joseph was sold to Potiphar, a captain of Pharaoh. Joseph worked hard and God blessed all that he did. But then one day Potiphar's wife told lies about Joseph. Potiphar threw Joseph in prison where he stayed a long time.

Years later Pharaoh had two strange dreams. He sent for Joseph.

Joseph told Pharaoh, "Your dreams mean that there will be a famine. Get ready for it."

Pharaoh made Joseph the governor of Egypt. He put Joseph in charge of collecting and storing food.

Seven years later, when famine came to the whole world, there was plenty of food to eat in Egypt.

One day Joseph saw his ten older brothers arrive at the palace in Egypt. They had come to buy food.

When they bowed to honor him, he knew God had made his dreams come true. At first Joseph didn't tell them who he was. Finally he said, "I am Joseph!" His brothers were speechless . . . and they looked frightened!

Joseph said, "Don't be afraid or upset about what you did to me. I'm not going to hurt you. You sold me into slavery, but it was really God who sent me to Egypt."

The famine lasted five more years, so Joseph told his brothers to bring their families to live in Egypt.

Joseph said, "You planned to harm me but God arranged everything to save all of your lives!"

What Does This Mean for You?

To Think About

- What a shock for Joseph to be sold by his brothers! No good could possibly come from that, could it?

- Think about Joseph's troubles. Name some good reasons why God let Joseph be sold as a slave.

- Think about Joseph's attitude as a slave and in jail. When Joseph had a good attitude, God blessed him.

- What is *your* attitude when you face problems and difficulties? In what ways should your attitude change?

- What do you do when things go wrong in your life?

- Why can you be sure that God will work everything out for your good?

ALWAYS REMEMBER

- If God allows you to experience troubles or hard times, try not to be upset. Trust God to work it for good.

- Whenever you face a problem, keep a thankful attitude. You can always be thankful that you belong to God no matter what happens.

- God promises to turn *all* things for good in your life. Everything will help you grow strong. It will all fit into God's good plan for your life.

God's Treasury of Promises

We know that in all things God works for the good
of those who love him.
Romans 8:28

Rejoice in the Lord always. . . . In everything, by prayer and
petition, with thanksgiving, present your requests to God.
Philippians 4:4, 6

Give thanks in all circumstances, for this is God's will for you
in Christ Jesus.
1 Thessalonians 5:18

Consider it pure joy, my brothers, whenever you face trials of
many kinds, because you know that the testing of your faith
develops perseverance.
James 1:2–3

Our fathers disciplined us for a little while as they thought
best; but God disciplines us for our good.
Hebrews 12:10

Chapter 14

Jesus' Promise: I Will Come Again!

Megan adjusted her ski boots and tightened the buckles of her cross-country skis. Then she pushed off, sliding forward on her skis through the snowy pines.

I was already at the end of the line. Now I've got to hurry to catch up with everyone else.

Megan was the youngest member at her family's reunion. All her relatives had longer skis—and longer legs—than she did!

"Here I come!" she called to her parents.

But when she skied out of the forest, she saw only an empty trail ahead.

"Dad! Mom! Where are you? Wait for me!"

Suddenly the snow-covered mountain didn't look so exciting. Without her family, Megan felt so alone and frightened.

How did everyone get so far ahead of me? she wondered.

Large snowflakes swirled around her. She knew the ski trail would be covered with snow in minutes.

Pulling her green knit hat down over her ears, she pumped her legs and arms and skied as fast as she could. She had to hurry.

I don't even know if I'm still on the right trail. Do my parents know I'm missing?

As she skied, she prayed, "Dear Lord, what should I do?"

Tears clouded her vision. The trail was fast disappearing. She knew she was lost.

Then, almost as though someone had said it, a thought popped into her mind: *Wait here for help.*

Megan stopped. "Where did that come from?" she asked herself. Trembling with cold and fear, she thought about what she had heard. Should she pay attention to the words?

The thought came again: *Wait here. They will return for you.* A warm blanket of peace settled over Megan.

"Of course," Megan said. "My folks will return for me. They won't leave me out here alone." Then another thought came to Megan's mind: *Sing and dance your praises to me.*

"Dear Lord, is that what you want me to do?" Megan prayed. "Okay. It doesn't do any good to worry, so I'll praise you. I'll stay right here and dance all around. I know you've heard my cry for help. You'll bring my parents back to find me."

Megan unbuckled her skis and leaned them against a pine tree. She lifted her arms up high and began to twirl and sing, making up her own song to Jesus. She sang and danced while the shadows deepened and night fell.

All during that snowy night, Megan joyfully sang and danced her praises to Jesus. What she didn't know was that the movement was keeping her from freezing to death.

Finally the snow stopped and the stars sparkled in the clear sky. As she sang, Megan thought of that special star long ago that led the wise men to Jesus.

And somehow Megan felt more certain than ever that her parents would return.

By the time a pink-and-gold sunrise lit up the mountain peaks, Megan was very, very cold. Then she heard a helicopter! When it came into view, she waved her hat wildly. She shouted, "Thank you, Jesus!"

The helicopter circled above her, then dipped low. Sure enough, there were her parents on board. They grinned and waved. Megan jumped up and down, wildly waving her arms in the air.

"They've seen me! They know where I am!"

She saw the helicopter landing in a field nearby, and soon her parents came skiing around the bend. She ran to them as fast as she could and hugged them, saying, "I just *knew* you'd return!"

What About You?

Have you ever gotten separated from your parents? It was terrifying, wasn't it?

But you probably knew they would be looking for you, didn't you?

Do you ever look up in the puffy clouds and think about Jesus returning to earth?

What makes a person ready for Jesus' return?

This is a good time to ask yourself these questions:
"Am I expecting Jesus to return?"
"Am I ready for Jesus to return?"

Jesus loves you. You can trust him to keep every promise he makes.

But there is one promise Jesus made that hasn't happened yet. He promised that he would return to earth once again—this time with power and glory!

Now he wants you to look forward to his return.

Jesus told his friends, "My coming will not be hidden. I will be seen by everyone on earth. It will be like lightning that comes from the east and can be seen in the west."

Jesus Promised He Would Return
Matthew 24-25

One day the disciples came to Jesus and asked, "What will be the sign of your coming?"

Jesus answered, "Many will claim to be the Messiah sent from God. Don't believe them.

"You will hear about wars, but don't be afraid. Future wars must happen.

"Great troubles are going to come upon the earth. People will be hungry. Many will starve. Earthquakes will strike in many different places. But do not be upset or afraid."

Jesus then told them a story about ten bridesmaids. They knew that the bridegroom would be coming to get his bride. But they didn't know when he would arrive.

All the girls brought lamps, but only five brought extra oil. They waited a long time, but still the groom did not come. Finally all ten of them fell asleep.

At midnight a voice cried out, "Here's the groom! Come meet him!"

The girls woke up and trimmed the wicks on their lamps. They needed the light on the dark path as they followed the groom.

Now the five foolish girls discovered they didn't have enough oil. "Give us some of your oil," they demanded. "Our lamps are going out."

But the wise girls said, "If we give you some of our oil, then we won't have enough to last the night."

So the foolish girls went to buy more oil. While they were gone, the groom arrived at the bride's house and everyone went in to the wedding party.

When the foolish girls arrived, they pounded on the door. But the groom would not let them in, because they had not been ready.

Jesus warned his friends, "Keep watch! You also must be ready. I will return at an hour when you don't expect me. No one knows that hour. Only the heavenly Father knows."

What Does This Mean for You?

To Think About

- Read the promise Jesus made: "Everyone will see me when I return on the clouds of the sky. I will come with power and with great glory. I will send my angels with a loud trumpet call. They will gather all of my people from every direction."

- Can you imagine how exciting it will be to hear the sound of a trumpet, watch the sky open up, and see Jesus coming in all his glory with millions of angels?

- Are you ready to meet him face-to-face?

- Have you asked Jesus to be your Savior?

- Have you asked his forgiveness? (If not, stop and do it right now!)

ALWAYS REMEMBER

- Jesus first came to earth as a helpless baby. But when he returns, he will come with power and great glory!

- Wait and always be *ready* for Jesus to return. Expect him any day. Don't stop praying. Don't give up on doing what is right.

- You are *ready* for Jesus to return when you ask his forgiveness and trust him as your Savior.

GOD'S TREASURY OF PROMISES

Keep watch, because you do not know
on what day your Lord will come.
Matthew 24:42

All the nations of the earth . . . will see the Son of Man
coming on the clouds of the sky, with power and great glory.
Matthew 24:30

Jesus said, "Behold, I am coming soon! . . . I am . . . the
Beginning and the End."
Revelation 22:12 – 13

The Lord himself will come down from heaven, with a loud
command, with the voice of the archangel and with the
trumpet call of God.
1 Thessalonians 4:16

Two angels told Jesus' disciples, "Jesus, who has been taken
from you into heaven, will come back in the same way you
have seen him go into heaven."
Acts 1:11

Chapter 15

God's Promise:
I Will Reward
You for What You
Have Done

"HEY! WAIT A MINUTE!" shouted John.

He and his friend Andrew slid sideways on their bikes as they braked to a stop.

Dropping his bike in the gravel, John rushed over to a red Buick parked on a side street. He got down on his hands and knees. Reaching his arm under the front of the car, he retrieved the black lump he had seen when he turned the corner.

"Look! It's a wallet!" he said triumphantly, lifting up the leather pouch. "And it feels full!"

Andrew got off his bike and reached out to grab the wallet. "Let me see!" he ordered.

John turned his back, pulling the wallet close.

"Come on. Show me what's inside," begged Andrew as he laid his bike down on the ground.

Keeping an eye on Andrew, John cautiously opened the wallet. He let out a low whistle.

"Wow! There's money inside—a lot of it!"

"I'll count it for you," offered Andrew with a grin.

"No way!" John flipped through the bills, adding them up. His eyes widened.

"You won't believe this!" he told Andrew in a hushed whisper. "There's over three hundred dollars in here! I've never held that much money—I'm rich!"

John thought about all the things he could buy with three hundred dollars.

Andrew was also silent for a moment. "Finders keepers," he said. "If we're the ones who found this, we should be able to keep it."

John frowned. "We? Hey—tell me again who found it. It was *me,* not you! Why should I have to share this money with you?"

"I thought we were best friends!" said Andrew. "But I see you're more interested in keeping the money yourself than in sharing!"

Both boys glared at each other for a moment.

"Check to see if there is any identification in the wallet," said Andrew. "You can't return it if there's no name or address inside it."

John's fingers trembled as he looked through the wallet. Then he found a driver's license.

"Well, it's here," said John. "The man's address and his phone number are here, also.

These must be some photos of his family." He sighed. "There goes the new bike I need."

Andrew thought for a moment. "I'll bet the owner doesn't know exactly how much money is here. Maybe we need to keep a little . . . as a reward for finding it."

"It would be easy to keep some," said John. "Most kids who found this would probably help themselves."

For a moment John considered the idea. "I know Jesus would give it all back," he said. "We'll feel better if we give it all back, too. Let's call the owner."

John phoned the number in the wallet. The man was the owner of the store where the car had been parked. The wallet had fallen out of his coat pocket when he hurried into his store that morning.

The man asked them to drop off the wallet at his store. "The money doesn't matter to me," he said on the phone. "It's the pictures inside that are so valuable."

"One picture is of my parents, who died in an accident when I was a little boy. It's the only photo I have of them!"

John and Andrew rode their bikes to the store—it was a bicycle shop. They handed the wallet to the store owner. He thanked them and they turned to leave.

"Wait!" he said. He waved his arm toward the display of bikes in his store. "Bring your parents with you tomorrow. I'll let each of you pick out a dirt bike you'd like. I want to reward you!"

On the way home John said to Andrew, "We only did what was right. Now he's giving us a greater reward than we imagined!"

What About You?

What a find—a wallet with over three hundred dollars! Yet that didn't match the reward both boys got in the end—two expensive bikes, plus the joy of helping someone.

Have you ever received a reward for something you've done? Tell about it.

Have you ever rewarded anyone else for something they have done for you? What did you give them?

What kind of rewards do you think God gives?

Think about the twelve men who left everything to follow Jesus—their jobs, homes, money, and families. Did the twelve disciples ever wonder if they would receive a reward? Yes, they did.

Jesus said, "When the Son of Man sits on his glorious throne, you who have followed me will also sit on twelve thrones, judging the twelve tribes of Israel. And everyone who has left houses or brothers or sisters or father or mother or children or fields for my sake will receive a hundred times as much and will inherit eternal life" (Matthew 19:27–29).

The King Returns and Gives Out Rewards
Matthew 25

Jesus told his disciples a special story about rewards. He said, "The Son of Man will come in all his glory. All the angels will come with him. Then he will sit on his throne in the glory of heaven.

"All the nations will be gathered in front of him. He will separate the people into two groups. He will be like a shepherd who separates the sheep from the goats. He will put the sheep to his right and the goats to his left.

"Then the King will speak to those on his right.

"The King will say, 'My Father has blessed you. Come and take what is yours. It is the kingdom prepared for you since the world was created.

"'I was hungry. And you gave me something to eat.

"'I was thirsty. And you gave me something to drink.

"'I was a stranger. And you invited me in.

"'I needed clothes. And you gave them to me.

"'I was sick. And you took care of me.

"'I was in prison. And you came to visit me.'

"'Then the people who have done what is right will answer him.

"'Lord,' they will ask, 'when did we see you hungry and feed you? When did we see you thirsty and give you something to drink?

"'When did we see you as a stranger and invite you in? When did we see you needing clothes and give them to you? When did we see you sick or in prison and go to visit you?'

"The King will reply, 'What I'm about to tell you is true. Anything you did for one of the least important of these brothers of mine, you did for me.'"

Jesus said. "Don't do good deeds to be seen by others and praised by them.... Your Father in heaven will reward you. He sees everything you do secretly."

What Does This Mean for You?

To Think About

- Why do you think God would reward us for doing good to others? Isn't that what we are supposed to do?

- What does it mean to be secret about your giving? Why shouldn't you tell other people about the good things you do?

- Why do you think God wants you to be generous, especially to poor people and to little children?

- God is the Creator of everything! What kinds of rewards could God give to us?

ALWAYS REMEMBER

- Heaven is a gift of God, not a reward for doing good. But God does promise to reward you in heaven for all the good you've done here on earth.

- God sees everything. Even when others don't notice or appreciate what you do, God sees it all. And God will reward you for everything—even giving a child some water.

- God wants you to be especially generous to people who cannot repay you. Treat everyone the way you would treat Jesus. He accepts everything you do as done to himself.

GOD'S TREASURY OF PROMISES

He who is kind to the poor lends to the LORD, and he will
reward him for what he has done.
Proverbs 19:17

Jesus said, "If anyone gives even a cup of cold water to one
of these little ones because he is my disciple . . .
he will certainly not lose his reward."
Matthew 10:42

Love your enemies, do good to them, and lend to them
without expecting to get anything back.
Then your reward will be great.
Luke 6:35

Jesus said, "I am coming soon! My reward is with me, and I
will give to everyone according to what he has done."
Revelation 22:12

When you give a banquet, invite the poor, the crippled,
the lame, the blind, and you will be blessed.
Although they cannot repay you, you will be repaid
at the resurrection of the righteous.
Luke 14:13—14

Chapter 16

God's Promise: I Will Give You a Home in Heaven

Brittany climbed up on the kitchen stool while her father finished cooking supper. The house seemed so quiet without her mother and all the friends who had helped during her mother's illness.

She frowned as her father handed her a plate of pasta and vegetables. Using her fork, she picked out all the pieces of broccoli and shoved them to one corner of her plate.

"Daddy, what kind of food will God serve in heaven?" she asked. "Will it taste good?"

"I don't think you have to worry about that," said Dad. "God probably serves the tastiest meals."

"Good! I don't want Mommy to have to eat broccoli. She didn't like it, either."

"Do people cry in heaven?" Brittany asked her father while they ate. "Do they get sick? Will people ever die again?"

"There are no tears or death or sickness in heaven." Dad tickled her under the chin. "In heaven you're going to laugh and sing and giggle more than you ever have before."

"Will I get tired of being happy all the time?"

Dad laughed. "I don't think so. You'll be having too much fun."

"Will it be like our vacation at the beach?"

"Maybe," said Dad. "Think about all the fun times we have here on earth. I'm sure good times will be even *better* in heaven."

Brittany silently helped clear off the dinner table. Tears filled her eyes.

"I didn't like it when we had to tell Mommy good-bye," she said softly. "I didn't want her to leave."

"Neither did I," said Dad in a quiet voice.

"When Mommy kissed me good-bye, she told me that she'd be waiting for me at heaven's gate."

"Yes," said Dad. "She wanted you to know that we would see her again. And she didn't want you to be afraid when it's your turn to go to heaven. She's there waiting for you . . . and me."

"When will I get to see heaven?" asked Brittany.

"I don't know," said Dad. "God is the one who decides when it is time to take us to his home in heaven."

That night Dad knelt by Brittany's bed to pray.

"I love you, Daddy," she whispered. "But I wish Mommy was here."

"I do, too, honey. But I love you, and I'll take care of you the best I can." He gently stroked her cheek. "Do you remember what Mommy prayed before she died?" he asked.

Brittany nodded. "She asked Jesus to take good care of me. And she asked him to bring us all to heaven someday—at the right time."

Brittany knew she would miss her mother. But she also knew Jesus was with her. And she knew that someday they would all be together— in heaven. God had promised.

What About You?

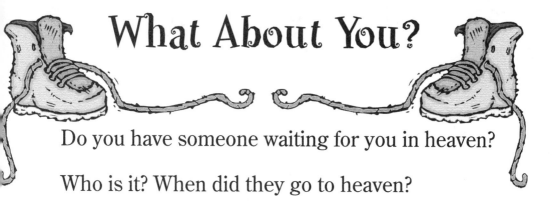

Do you have someone waiting for you in heaven?

Who is it? When did they go to heaven?

Have you ever wondered what heaven will be like?

Would God make a good home for us?

We know heaven will be a great place to live. And it probably will be full of wonderful surprises because Jesus promised to get it ready for us.

Just think about the fun activities to do here on earth. What are some things you enjoy?

What do you hope heaven will be like?

What's the first thing you want to tell Jesus when you see him?

What About You?

What will you ask him?

Can you remember some people in the Bible who looked into heaven? Isaiah, Daniel, and Ezekiel all saw a glimpse of God in heaven (Isaiah 6:1–10; Daniel 7:9–14; Ezekiel 1:25–28).

Before Stephen (a follower of Jesus) died, he saw a vision of heaven. He told everyone that he saw Jesus standing at God's right hand (Acts 7:54–60).

Have you read John's vision of when he was taken up from earth and given a special look into heaven? He wrote it all down for us in the last book of the Bible—the book of Revelation.

John's vision of heaven will make you excited about God's wonderful home, where you will live forever!

God Gave John a Look into Heaven
Revelation 1, 7, 21, 22

The Roman rulers had ordered John, the youngest of Jesus' twelve disciples, to stop telling everyone about Jesus. But John would not stop.

So the Romans sent John away to live on a small island. There, God gave him a heavenly vision.

John wrote, "I heard a loud voice that sounded like a trumpet. The voice said, 'Write down what you see. Send it out to other Christians.'"

John saw a door standing open in the sky. He saw a throne in heaven, circled with a rainbow. The One who sat on the throne was shining like jewels.

"Millions and millions of angels" gathered around the throne and sang praise to God.

John wrote, "There was a huge crowd of people—so many that no one could count them.

They came from every nation, tribe, people, and language. They were wearing white robes."

The crowd praised God with loud voices.

An angel told John, "They have washed their robes and made them white in the blood of Jesus, the Lamb."

John saw the beautiful Holy City. There were twelve gates in the city, each made of a single pearl. An angel stood at each gate.

The city and its streets were made out of pure gold, as clear as glass. Its walls were decorated with valuable jewels of every color.

God will wipe away every tear from the people's eyes. There will be no more death or sadness. There will be no more crying or pain. Things are no longer the way they used to be.

The angel showed John the river of the water of life. It was as clear as crystal. It flowed from Jesus and from the throne of God down the city's main street. On both sides of the river stood the tree of life, full of fruit.

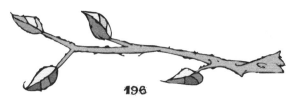

What Does This Mean for You?

To Think About

- Why is heaven a wonderful place?

- In what ways will life in heaven be different from life here on earth?

- What are you looking forward to doing in heaven?

- What do you think it will be like not to have any pain or sadness or nighttime?

- Why can you be sure that God will take you to heaven?

ALWAYS REMEMBER

- If life on earth can be fun and exciting, you can be sure heaven will be even more joyful and exciting!

- Life here on earth does not last very long. Life in heaven lasts forever. Whenever you experience the death of a loved one, remind yourself that your real home is in heaven!

- Heaven is a gift from God. It is given to every person who puts their trust in Jesus as their Savior.

GOD'S TREASURY OF PROMISES

I will dwell in the house of the Lord forever.
Psalm 23:6

Jesus said, "In my Father's house are many rooms. . . . I am going there to prepare a place for you. And if I go and prepare a place for you, I will come back and take you to be with me that you also may be where I am."
John 14:2–3

Our citizenship is in heaven. And we eagerly await a Savior from there, the Lord Jesus Christ.
Philippians 3:20

God will wipe every tear from their eyes. There will be no more death or mourning or crying or pain.
Revelation 21:4

No eye has seen, no ear has heard, no mind has conceived what God has prepared for those who love him.
1 Corinthians 2:9

Chapter 17

God's Promise: I Will Keep Every Promise

Jody grabbed the rails of the ladder leading to the high diving board. She tried to concentrate on climbing one step at a time.

"Go ahead, Jody!" her father's strong voice reassured her. "I'll be right down here in the water waiting for you. I know you can do it! Don't worry."

Jody paused halfway up the ladder. Looking down gave her goose bumps. The new Olympic-sized diving board seemed to tower a mile above the pool.

I can't do this! she thought. Her knuckles grew white as she tightened her grip on the rails.

That morning Dad had assured her, "You're a great swimmer, Jody. Believe me—you're good enough to jump off the big diving board. The first time is always a little scary, but you can do it! And I'll be there."

She could see her dad treading water in the deep end. He smiled and waved one arm at her.

"Don't stop climbing!" called her father. "You'll be just fine. I'll swim up close to you when you dive. I promise."

Jody felt more confident as he spoke. She knew her dad wouldn't let her jump off the big board unless he knew it would be all right.

Reaching the top of the ladder, Jody pulled herself up on the board. She looked out over the pool. Was everyone looking at her? Could they see her shivering?

Down below, her dad waited. She knew he wouldn't let anything happen to her. If she panicked and swallowed too much water, he would reach out and rescue her. He had done that once before when she was three years old. She had jumped off the side of the pool but couldn't swim. He had pulled her from the bottom of the pool and saved her life.

"Go ahead, Jody. I'm here to help you," he called.

Jody glanced at the ladder. No one was behind her. It would be easy to climb back down.

Jody looked again at her father. Without him being there, she didn't have enough courage to jump. But she knew she could trust him.

She walked slowly to the edge of the board. It bent slightly under her weight. Taking a deep breath, she held her nose, closed her eyes, and jumped.

Down she fell. It seemed like forever until her body plunged into the cool water. Kicking and pulling at the water with her arms, she shot back up to the surface. She emerged sputtering and gasping for breath.

Her dad reached out a strong arm to steady her while she caught her breath. She relaxed in his grip. He was there to help—just as he'd promised.

What About You?

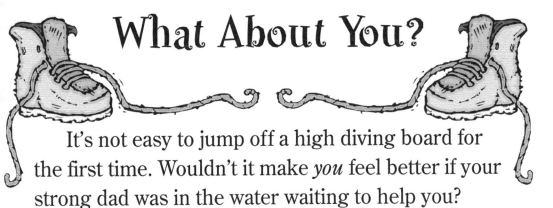

It's not easy to jump off a high diving board for the first time. Wouldn't it make *you* feel better if your strong dad was in the water waiting to help you?

When have you had to trust someone's promise?

Stop and think about a time when you knew you couldn't do something by yourself. Did someone else promise to help you?

Did they keep their promise?

How did you feel when they did (or didn't) do what they said they would do?

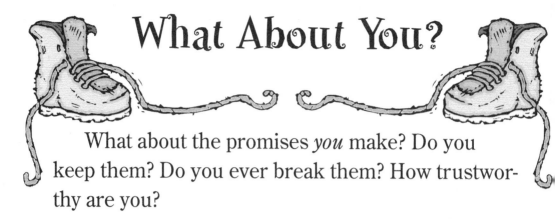

What About You?

What about the promises *you* make? Do you keep them? Do you ever break them? How trustworthy are you?

Can you think of some situations in the Bible in which people had to trust God for help?

When God spoke to Noah about sending a flood, it was hard for Noah to imagine what was going to happen. But God gave Noah all the instructions for building a big boat. It was large enough to keep him and his family safe, along with many birds and lots of other animals.

Noah believed that God would send a flood, just as God had said. And Noah believed God's promise to save him. So he spent many years building the ark. All the while, he trusted God's promise.

God's Promise to Noah
Genesis 6:8-9:17

Many years ago God came to Noah and said, "People have filled the earth with hatred and violence. I am going to send a flood on the earth to destroy every living creature. Make an ark.

"I will make my covenant with you. [A covenant is a very serious and important promise.] Take your family and a male and a female of every living creature into the ark."

Noah did everything the Lord told him to do.

When the flood began, the waters rose higher. They lifted the ark high above the earth. The ark floated on the water.

Every living creature on earth died except those with Noah.

It took many months for the water to go down and for the earth to dry. At last Noah's ark came to rest on the top of a mountain. Then Noah and his family stepped outside. The birds and animals followed them.

The first thing Noah did was to build an altar of stones. On it he sacrificed some of the extra birds and animals he had taken on the ark.

This was Noah's way of saying thank you to God for keeping all of them safe.

Then God promised Noah, "I will never again send a flood to cover the earth and destroy all life. As long as the earth endures, there will always be seedtime and harvest, summer and winter, day and night."

God made another covenant with Noah. "Here is the sign of the covenant I am making," said God. "I have put my rainbow in the clouds."

Let the rainbow be a reminder to you that God is the greatest promise-maker . . . and the greatest promise-keeper.

What Does This Mean for You?

To Think About

- Why, do you think, would God give promises to you?

- Think about some of the promises of God that you can remember.

- What does a rainbow mean to you?

- After reading this chapter, what promises of God will you remember when you see a rainbow?

ALWAYS REMEMBER

- God only makes promises that he is able to keep. You can always trust what God says.

- God is trustworthy. Even if you can't trust anyone else, you can trust your faithful God. History proves that God keeps every promise.

- God has a special way and a special time for keeping promises. Don't give up if you have to wait. You can be sure God is always on time and never late.

GOD'S TREASURY OF PROMISES

God who promised is faithful.
Hebrews 10:23

The Lord is not slow in keeping his promise.
2 Peter 3:9

When you have done the will of God,
you will receive what he has promised.
Hebrews 10:36

Not one of all the good promises the Lord your God gave you
has failed. Every promise has been fulfilled.
Joshua 23:14

Trust in the Lord with all your heart. . . . the Lord will be your
confidence and will keep your foot from being snared.
Proverbs 3:5, 26

God who was seated on the throne . . . said, "Write this down,
for these words are trustworthy and true."
Revelation 21:5

Chapter 18

God's Promise:
I Will Reward
Your Faith

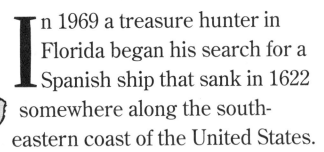

In 1969 a treasure hunter in Florida began his search for a Spanish ship that sank in 1622 somewhere along the south-eastern coast of the United States.

This man was very interested in finding the sunken ship. He had read in old shipping records that this ship had been carrying a large cargo of gold and silver.

For over two hundred years, a lot of people had tried to discover where the ship sank. But no one ever found it.

While the man in Florida searched, many people laughed at him. They thought the treasure hunter was wasting his time reading through all the old record books he could find.

But the man did not give up his search. He believed that he would someday be able to find out exactly where the ship sank. So he kept studying what had been recorded about the ship's course and its destination. He finally figured out that the ship had to have been sailing off the coast of Florida when it sank.

He spent a lot of money using many different boats and different ways to "look" at the bottom of the ocean.

Then in 1985, after sixteen long years of searching, the treasure hunter and his crew thought they saw something big in the deep water off the Florida coast.

With the help of sonar sound waves, they finally located an object that appeared to be the remains of a ship. Everyone got excited!

When the crew had determined the exact spot where the sunken ship lay, divers were sent down to the bottom of the ocean. They looked around and inside the wreckage of the old ship.

When they came back up to the surface of the water, they showed the treasure hunter many samples of the gold and silver and jewels which were still aboard the ship.

And the treasure hunter found out that what he had believed all along was really true. Even though the old ship had fallen apart, its fantastic treasure was still there! The whole crew celebrated their success.

After all the cargo was salvaged from the sunken ship, they estimated what the gold and silver was worth. It was valued at forty million dollars—far more than anyone had expected!

What a treasure! What an incredible find!

Do you think he was glad he hadn't stopped searching all those years? Do you think he was glad he hadn't listened to the people who said it couldn't be done?

Yes! His "faith" was greatly rewarded. He wasn't sorry for spending all those years and all his money to find the amazing treasure of gold and silver and jewels.

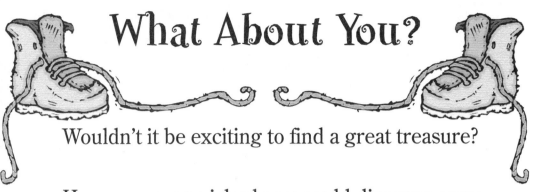

What About You?

Wouldn't it be exciting to find a great treasure?

Have you ever wished you could discover something valuable while digging in your backyard?

Even if you never find gold or silver, you can be sure God's treasure won't be hard for you to discover. But it will take effort on your part ... and time.

Remember: God and his treasury of promises are worth more than a ship full of jewels. God and his promises last forever.

Would you be able to pay for God's love or forgiveness?

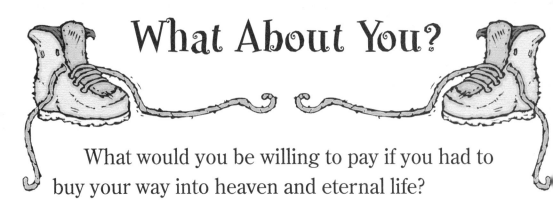

What About You?

What would you be willing to pay if you had to buy your way into heaven and eternal life?

In the books of Matthew, Mark, Luke, and John, you will read about many people who trusted Jesus.

Sick people were brought to him because they had faith that he would heal them. Sometimes Jesus told them, "Your faith has made you well."

Blind men called out to Jesus until he stopped to help them. They had faith that he could heal their sight.

Jesus spent three years teaching his disciples to trust him. Now read about two times when Peter and the other disciples learned what it meant to live in faith.

Living in Faith
Matthew 14:22-32

Late one afternoon Jesus told his disciples to sail across the Sea of Galilee. They left and Jesus went up a hill to pray alone.

By evening a storm came up. The wind blew hard. Waves pounded the boat. The disciples were terrified.

Then, early in the morning, Jesus walked out on the water to the disciples' boat. When they saw him walking on the lake, they were sure it was a ghost.

Jesus called to them, "Be brave! It is I. Don't be afraid."

"Lord, is it really you?" asked Peter. "If it is, tell me to come to you on the water."

"Come," Jesus said.

So Peter climbed out of the boat. With his eyes on Jesus, he walked on the water. But suddenly Peter felt a gust of wind push against him. He took his eyes off

Jesus. Looking out at the roaring, pounding waves, Peter felt afraid. He began to sink into the deep lake.

Peter stretched out his hand. "Lord! Save me!"

Right away Jesus reached out and grabbed Peter's hand. "Your faith is so small!" Jesus said. "Why did you doubt me?" He led Peter back to the boat. When they climbed in, the wind died down. All the disciples worshiped Jesus and said, "You are the Son of God!"

Another time Jesus saw a fig tree beside the road. He went to get some figs to eat. The tree had no figs.

Jesus said to the tree, "May you never bear fruit again!" And the tree just dried up!

When the disciples asked how this could happen, Jesus said, "You must have faith and not doubt," Then you can do what was done to the fig tree. And you can say to this mountain, 'Go and throw yourself into the sea.' And it will be done."

Jesus told them, "If you believe and have faith, you will receive what you ask for when you pray."

Remember: this promise of Jesus is still true for you today!

What Does This Mean for You?

To Think About

- Think about what it means to have faith in Jesus.

- Do you believe Jesus can do the impossible?

- Do you ever pray for "impossible" things and trust him to help you?

- When have you had faith to trust Jesus?

- When have you doubted that Jesus would answer your prayers, take care of you, or help you in times of trouble?

ALWAYS REMEMBER

- Jesus wants you to live *by faith*. Will you trust him even when you feel disappointed and when it seems he has let you down?

- Jesus wants your faith to grow. What makes your faith deepen and grow? (Do you read your Bible and pray? Do you take time to be alone with Jesus?)

- Jesus wants you to live a life of faith. You can trust that he will answer every prayer and bring you victory over every trouble. Nothing is impossible *if* you trust him.

GOD'S TREASURY OF PROMISES

Faith is being sure of what we hope for and certain
of what we do not see.
Hebrews 11:1

Jesus said, "If you believe, you will receive
whatever you ask for in prayer."
Matthew 21:22

When a man asks in prayer, he must believe and not doubt.
James 1:6

Jesus told Martha, "Did I not tell you that if you believed,
you would see the glory of God?"
John 11:40

Do not throw away your confidence; it will be richly
rewarded. You need to persevere so that when you have done
the will of God, you will receive what he has promised.
Hebrews 10:35–36